mindful
RELATIONSHIPS

Dr Richard Chambers is a clinical psychologist in private practice, specializing in mindfulness-based therapies, and an internationally recognized expert in mindfulness. Dr Chambers is pioneering a university-wide mindfulness approach at Melbourne's Monash University and consults to a growing number of educational institutions, businesses, sporting clubs and community organizations. He is a developer of the Smiling Mind app and co-author of *Mindful Learning*, also by Exisle.

Margie Ulbrick is a collaborative family lawyer, relationship counsellor, psychotherapist and writer. Trained in Family Therapy, Somatic Therapy, Law and Collaborative Practice, she has many years' experience working to help people create sustaining and nurturing relationships and work towards maximizing optimum health in families. As a relationship counsellor, Margie works with couples, individuals and families, and teaches the skills of mindfulness to assist in promoting healthy relationships. In her roles as a collaborative family lawyer and communications coach, she works to create the best possible outcome for families going through separation and divorce. Margie's articles have been published on websites and in journals, newspapers and magazines.

mindful
RELATIONSHIPS

Creating genuine connection with ourselves and others

Dr Richard Chambers and Margie Ulbrick

EXISLE
PUBLISHING

First published 2016

Exisle Publishing Pty Ltd
'Moonrising', Narone Creek Road, Wollombi, NSW 2325, Australia
P.O. Box 60–490, Titirangi, Auckland 0642, New Zealand
www.exislepublishing.com

A CiP record for this book is available from the National Library of Australia.

ISBN 978 1 921966 78 1

Designed by Christabella Designs
Illustration on page 27 courtesy of Shutterstock
Typeset in Bembo 11.5/18
Printed in China

This book uses paper sourced under ISO 14001 guidelines from well-managed forests and other controlled sources.

10 9 8 7 6 5 4 3 2 1

Disclaimer
While this book is intended as a general information resource and all care has been taken in compiling the contents, neither the authors nor the publisher and their distributors can be held responsible for any loss, claim or action that may arise from reliance on the information contained in this book. As each person and situation is unique, it is the responsibility of the reader to consult a qualified professional regarding their personal circumstances.

CONTENTS

Part 1: Mindfulness as relationship   1

1. Mindfulness as relationship   3

2. What is mindfulness?   9

3. The science of mindful relationships   25

Part 2: The mindful self   37

4. How to meditate   39

5. Applying mindfulness   51

Part 3: The mindful couple   69

6. Intimacy   71

7. Healthy relationships   85

8. Mindful sex   105

9. When things go wrong   117

10. Seeking help   131

Part 4: The mindful family   139

11. Mindful parenting   141

12. Raising mindful children   157

13. Creating a mindful family   171

Part 5: The mindful workplace   185

14. Working mindfully   187

15. Mindfulness at work and in groups   195

16. Mindful leadership   203

Epilogue: Creating a mindful society   215

Endnotes   222

Index   229

PART 1

Mindfulness as relationship

CHAPTER 1
Mindfulness as relationship

Mindfulness *is* relationship. It is our relationship with ourselves and the world around us. With each breath, each thought, each moment. It is how we experience our bodies and emotions, and how we relate to one another. Cultivating mindfulness gives us the ability to be present and nonreactive. Later, we discover the importance of being gentle and friendly toward ourselves, which improves our wellbeing and overall functioning. Mindfulness becomes heartfulness, and a whole new way of relating to ourselves, and the world, begins to unfold.

Even though mindfulness starts off being a very personal journey, when we start to really grasp what it is, it naturally becomes about others. As we rediscover our innate curiosity we start to notice the people and the world around us with fresh eyes, rather than reacting to them in conditioned, habitual ways. We start to see new possibilities and space where before we perceived only fixed patterns of relating. We see that the difficulties we face as individuals are the same difficulties faced by everyone, everywhere. Reactivity, stress, disconnection, unhappiness and illness are universal. At the same time, we see that the presence, curiosity, friendliness and compassion we can rediscover in ourselves through mindfulness practice can also be rediscovered by those around us.

Mindfulness ripples out from our centre. As we become more present, calmer and compassionate, these qualities flow out from us, first to the people we are closest to, then to everyone around us. And as anyone who has come into contact with someone who truly embodies aware presence knows, it has an immediate effect on us. Simply being around someone who exudes qualities of mindfulness from the core of their being connects us with these same qualities in ourselves. And in the very same way, when we start to embody mindfulness ourselves, the ripples inspire and transform everyone with whom we come into contact. These people then go on to inspire and enliven others and the process spreads out even further. It eventually comes back to us.

This book is about mindfulness *as* relationship. It explores what it means to develop a mindful relationship with ourselves and others. It is structured in a way that we first explore how to rediscover qualities of mindfulness such as presence, curiosity, love and compassion and develop intimacy with ourselves. We then go on to explore how we can bring these very qualities to all our relationships — increasing our intimacy with those around us, starting with our romantic partners and spouses, our children and other family members, our colleagues, neighbours and communities, and eventually society and the planet as a whole.

Throughout this book you will meet a number of real people who have undergone transformation personally and in their relationships through practising and applying mindfulness. These are people who have seen us for therapy or participated in our mindfulness courses.[1] It is our hope that their stories will bring to life the principles and practices that we explore and inspire you to use them in your own life. We also explore what the scientific evidence says about the benefits of mindfulness practice both for individuals and in relationships. The book is also filled with practical exercises so that you can start applying mindfulness right now, in your own life, by recognizing and changing relational patterns that limit intimacy and get in the way of having the relationships you want. We recommend that you read this book slowly, reflecting on the ideas and experimenting with the practices. Even if you choose to read it quickly in one go, you might like to then re-read it, a little at a time, checking out the ideas and seeing what effect they have on your relationships and your life in general.

A fundamental principle of mindfulness is that nothing should be taken on face value. As we explore in detail, curiosity is a fundamental quality of mindfulness, and it is lost when we just believe something we read or hear without checking it out for ourselves. Instead, we recommend that the reader treat everything in this book as a guide and conduct their own inquiry into what is true for them. It is our hope that through reading about and applying the ideas in this book you will naturally and easily start to rediscover your own innate wisdom and transform your relationships in the ways that they need to be transformed. Or, as we will see, mindfulness can create a sense of *space* and loving presence in which your relationships start to transform themselves.

We wrote this book because the world is in need of healing. Rates of divorce are high and many people stay in relationships that are deeply unhappy. Huge numbers of people live cut off from their own inner world and then wonder why they cannot find intimacy with others. And this lack of intimacy — with ourselves and others — means that many people exist in a state of disconnection from their communities and the ecology of the planet, with increasingly obvious negative consequences. It is therefore our hope that this book will guide you, the reader, back into a genuine intimacy with yourself. It is designed to help you reconnect with the tender, vulnerable parts of yourself and learn to hold these with gentleness and love. Only then can you learn to do this with the people around you, rediscovering the importance of connection in the process. After all, we are social beings and require genuine connectedness in order to thrive.

We feel it is important to dispel right away any illusions that we, the authors of this book, have perfect relationships. We have both struggled and faced many of the same kinds of challenges our readers have. Relationships can be hard! The habits of reactivity that lead to difficulties and conflict in relationships are universal. They occur across genders, cultures, sexual preferences and even — believe it or not — happen to experienced mindfulness meditators, teachers and therapists.

When we begin down the path of mindfulness, it is natural to hope that one day, with enough practice, all of the difficulties and pain will simply cease to occur. Many of us wish that somehow we will become inoculated against the ups and downs of life, or find ways to detach from the emotions so that we become immune to the hurt that seems unavoidable in relationships. But as people ripen on the path of meditation and mindfulness, they come to realize that discomfort and difficulty are a part of life and cannot be avoided. Trying to do so leads to *spiritual bypassing* — the attempt to use mindfulness or other forms of meditation to somehow avoid or get around the difficulties that are an intrinsic part of the human experience. Experienced mindfulness practitioners — the ones that have stuck with it and are really starting to get it — recognize that the path to liberation is *through* the difficulties rather than around them (or away from them). Learning to embrace the fullness of life, what mindfulness pioneer Jon Kabat-Zinn calls the 'full catastrophe', with a sense of openness and gentleness — this is the path to liberation.

Throughout *Mindful Relationships* we repeatedly revisit two key themes. The first is that true intimacy must begin with ourselves. It requires that we become able to fully inhabit our body, to be able to sense and be with whatever we notice there. Only once we become intimate with ourselves can we hope to become intimate with others. The second key theme is that this intimacy then spreads out in ever-expanding ripples, first to our partner, children and other loved ones, and then to work colleagues, communities and society as a whole. Through this process, as Gandhi said, we must be the change we want to see in the world.

EXERCISE: OBSERVING YOUR RELATIONSHIP WITH YOURSELF AND THE WORLD AROUND YOU

To help bring to life what we have said so far in this chapter, take a moment to tune in to yourself. Tune in to your body, noticing the sensations that are there without judgement or trying to do anything with them. Tune in to your mind and notice the quality of your awareness — whether your mind is busy and tense, awake and clear or sleepy and dull. Again, just observe without judgement. Notice what emotions are present. Give the emotions a name if you can, although don't get too caught up trying to do this 'right'.

Now take a moment to tune in to the environment. Listen to the sounds happening around you, and notice the silence that is there too. Perhaps look around you and become aware of what you can see.

Now, notice your relationship with what is happening right now. Are you allowing everything to be as it is, or is there judgement and a sense of fighting with how things are? Even if your intention is simply to notice what is happening, you might, if you are very attentive, notice subtle layers of judgement and reaction. It can be good to remember that this is the default setting of the brain, and to give yourself permission for this to be happening.

And see if you can — even just for a moment — allow things to be exactly as they are, and bring an attitude of acceptance and friendliness to whatever is happening within and around you. Don't try to fix or change anything, or even to understand it. Simply recognize what is true, right now, in this moment. And see if you can notice the peace that comes with doing this.

CHAPTER 2

What is mindfulness?

In Chapter 1 we outlined how mindfulness *is* relationship, both with ourselves and with the people and the world around us. We realize that this might be a new way of thinking about mindfulness for many people, so in this chapter we tie this in with more familiar approaches to explaining what mindfulness is, as well as how it can be practised and applied.

Mindfulness is living in the present and acting with awareness. This allows us to respond rather than react. It refers to the experience of *being* in the present moment, and also includes a range of attention training practices (meditations), applications and cognitive exercises designed to enhance our ability to do this. This is an important distinction because, as we explore in depth throughout this book, mindfulness is both a very ordinary experience that we all dip in and out of throughout the day, as well as something that we can deliberately cultivate and practise. Mindfulness is much more than simple attention training. It is a whole way of being, and ultimately it is an experience of getting in touch with a limitless space of awareness that experiences everything and yet remains unchanged by it.

Mindfulness *is* relationship.

Mindfulness as an everyday experience

It is good to recognize that mindfulness is an everyday experience rather than some special state of mind or way of being. For instance, think about the last time you sat and watched the sun go down. There is a pretty good chance you felt a sense of wellbeing and relaxation — and possibly even experienced a sense of your mind expanding as you sat and gazed out at the horizon. Or perhaps when you go walking in nature, whether on hikes or just in the park with your dog, you experience this same sense of wellbeing. You aren't having to consciously push thoughts of work or unpaid bills from your mind, but are somehow just effortlessly in the present — engaged with the sights, sounds and sensations such as your feet on the ground and the breeze blowing over your skin. In moments like these, our attention just comes to rest naturally in the present as we engage more fully with what is happening around us.

Engaging our attention in the senses like this leads to enhanced wellbeing and a greater appreciation for life. Worries and concerns seem to just subside by themselves. This is why we naturally seek out experiences and activities that promote this. If you stop and think about it, there are countless things that can help us experience this. In addition to watching sunsets and being out in nature, there are obvious things such as meditation, yoga and Pilates. For many, playing or listening to music, watching films and reading for enjoyment, cooking, gardening or doing arts and crafts are things that tend to engage them in exactly the same way. Physical exercise is a time that many people report feeling more connected to their bodies and therefore to the present moment. Here, we are not talking about being on a treadmill in a gym, watching TV or reading a magazine while working out. Instead, we are talking about feeling the body move, being aware of its posture and breathing from moment to moment. Playing with children and pets also has a way of bringing us into the present moment, as they tend to naturally be quite present — and this invites us to do the same. The list is endless. In fact, if you think about your hobbies, there are probably things that engage your attention in the senses and lead to relaxation and wellbeing. We can find ourselves in 'flow' states, where we are effortlessly present and engaged. This is why we tend to seek these things out.

EXERCISE: RECOGNIZING WHEN WE ARE ALREADY MINDFUL

Take a moment to reflect on the things you do that engage your attention in the present. Think about this as broadly as possible and include things even if you only do them occasionally or for brief periods at a time. You might like to write a list of everything you can think of.

Now, reflect on how you feel while you are doing these things. You most likely feel relaxed and happy, since there is something inherently pleasant about being present and engaged. Perhaps make a commitment to yourself to build more of these things into your life so you can spend more time in the present. Notice the benefits of doing this.

You might even like to take a moment to notice yourself reading this book right now, and observe how this makes you feel.

Default mode

Our minds wander constantly. Researchers Matthew Killingsworth and Daniel Gilbert have found that our attention is off-task around 47 per cent of the time (unless making love, in which case those surveyed daydreamed a bit less).[1] Ask any mindfulness teacher or serious meditator, though, and they will tell you that the true figure is *way* more than this, suggesting that the people surveyed in Killingsworth and Gilbert's study might have been simply unaware just how much mind wandering was going on. This unconscious mind-wandering and mental chatter is commonly called 'default mode'. When we are in this mode, specific parts of the brain — known as the 'default mode network' — become active. And these brain areas are very different from the parts that are active when we are mindful.

Unsurprisingly, being in default mode can cause us problems. Killingsworth and Gilbert found that mind wandering makes us consistently less happy. They found that people whose attention was in the past or future were less happy overall than people who were focused on what they were doing. This was true even if they were thinking about pleasant things. The reason for this is that sometimes our attention wanders to something pleasant or useful, and can even lead to creativity, but this mind wandering strengthens the default-mode network, making it more likely that we will later get caught up in unpleasant, problematic mind wandering such as worrying, ruminating and reacting.

The reason it does this is not entirely clear, but being distractible and having a tendency to focus on problems probably had a survival advantage. We might imagine one of our ancestors 40,000 years ago hunting a mammoth. Their eyes might have been well and truly on the prize, when suddenly there was a rustling in the bushes nearby. It would have been useful for them to get distracted, even just momentarily, and wonder what might have made the noise. They would have also been much more likely to survive if they thought, 'That could be a sabre-toothed tiger, I'd better be careful!' than if they thought, 'Oh, it's probably just a rabbit.' These ancestors passed on to us a genetically determined 'negativity bias' where we notice and remember about seven times as many unpleasant things as positive ones. We are also much more likely to notice an unhappy face than a happy one.[2]

It's not hard to figure out who was more likely to survive long enough to procreate and pass on their genes to us. Forty thousand years later, life is a lot safer for most of us but we still have the same hardware in our heads that constantly scans the environment for threats. These days, these 'threats' tend to be things like deadlines, arguments, mistakes we have made and job interviews rather than actual threats to our physical safety.

There is a rapidly growing body of research showing that default mode is strongly associated with a range of mental and physical health problems such as anxiety, depression, Attention Deficit Hyperactivity Disorder (ADHD), Alzheimer's dementia and even schizophrenia and autism.[3,4,5,6,7,8] It is also associated with reduced academic and work performance, because if we aren't focused on the job we are doing we can't possibly be performing at our best.

And, as we will explore, the reactivity that tends to result from being in default mode has significant implications for our relationships — with both ourselves and others.

Automatic pilot

Closely related to default mode — in fact, we can more or less consider it the same thing — is automatic pilot. Ever noticed how much of the day you do things without really paying attention? For better or worse, once we have done something enough times to become familiar with it, we are able to do it automatically while thinking of something else. This can be a useful skill, for instance while walking down the street talking on the phone. But at times it can cause problems. Ever walked into your house and put your keys down while thinking about something else, then been unable to remember where your keys are when you want to leave again? Automatic pilot. And have you ever driven somewhere and been unable to recall the journey once you've arrived at your destination? Automatic pilot again. Obviously, driving around without paying attention can cause problems such as getting lost, accidents and road rage incidents as we get lost in reactivity. Eating on automatic pilot also causes problems. Ever been watching TV and looked down to find an empty pack of biscuits? As well as eating too much of the wrong types of food without listening to what our body really needs, the real tragedy is that we don't even taste the biscuits we are stuffing ourselves with! We can study, work and exercise on autopilot. The list is endless. And of course, when autopilot clicks on in our relationship, we end up not listening, saying things we later regret, getting into conflict and missing opportunities for connection and intimacy. Becoming aware of our autopilot tendencies is therefore crucial to having good relationships with ourselves and others.

Mindfulness as a practice

It is important to realize that default mode isn't inherently good or bad. It can lead to creativity or pleasant daydreams. However, it is important to be aware when we are in default mode. For instance, if we suddenly become aware that we are having a pleasant daydream and then realize that we are waiting for a train or lying in bed on a Sunday morning with nothing to do, we might want to keep daydreaming. By contrast, if the daydream is more of a nightmare — for instance, obsessing about some worry — or if we realize that we are actually at that moment sitting in an important meeting or driving on the freeway, we might want to bring our attention back to what we are doing! Mindfulness gives us the self-awareness — and therefore the capacity for choice — to do this.

As with anything, we become better at mindfulness the more we practise it. This is why mindfulness is often referred to as a 'practice'. Sometimes people refer to mindfulness 'exercises', which implies that regular training makes us stronger. This is true and, as we explore in the next chapter, practising mindfulness rewires the brain and literally builds a 'mindful muscle'. You have probably also heard the term 'mindfulness meditation'. 'Meditation' simply means 'attention training'. And mindfulness meditation begins with training the attention to be in the present moment by moment deliberately engaging with what is happening in the senses. As we become more and more present, we can start to turn awareness on itself and get into contact with a sense of being. This leads to an increased sense of wellbeing, as we become less reactive to what we experience. This is why, although mindfulness is not a religious practice in and of itself, it can be found at the heart of all contemplative religious traditions.

Practising mindfulness is conceptually very simple. It involves deliberately focusing the attention in the present by engaging it with something that is happening through the senses — seeing, hearing, feeling, smelling and tasting. Once we have learnt to do this, we can start bringing mindfulness to our thoughts and emotions. An important point is that it is not about trying to *stop* the mind wandering. As we have already said, we are wired to wander and trying to stop this will just give us a headache and make us think that mindfulness 'doesn't work'. Instead, the idea is to become better at recognizing when the mind has wandered. As we become better at recognizing it, we become quicker at bringing it back, especially when we do this non-judgementally and gently (important attitudes that we will discuss in a moment). The more we practise, the more the mind begins to settle. We soon find that we start spending longer periods engaged in the present. And when we cultivate this quality of attention through consistent practice, our brain starts to rewire itself and we start experiencing the same thing even when we are not meditating — when we are 'off the cushion', so to speak.

EXERCISE: USING YOUR BODY AS AN ANCHOR

Take a few moments to tune in to your body. Sit in a comfortable position. Simply notice how it feels, without judging or trying to change anything. It may help to close your eyes, so you can tune in more easily. Are you feeling tense? Relaxed? Tired? Simply notice what is happening there, remembering that there is no right or wrong. Mindfulness is simply about noticing what is true.

Then, take a moment to notice what is happening in your mind, again without judgement. Simply notice whether your mind is busy with thoughts, or relatively quiet, or sleepy and dull.

If you notice tension in the body, feel free to let it go. See if you can notice the actual muscles that are holding the tension and just start to release it. If the body relaxes, notice that. If it doesn't, simply notice that.

Likewise, if you notice mental tension — your mind wandering off into default mode — simply let it go and return your attention gently to your body.

Take a few moments just to sit and sense the body. Tune in to the pressure and support of the chair underneath you and the ground under your feet. Notice the tendency of the mind to wander off and simply keep bringing it gently back, practising patience as you do so.

Now, check in with your body once again and notice how it is feeling now. What is different compared to the start of the practice? Do you feel calmer and more relaxed? Have you learnt something about what is happening in your body and/or mind? Again, remember that there is no right or wrong. Just notice what is actually happening.

When you are ready, open your eyes (if they were closed) and notice what it is like to be a bit more present.

Informal practice

To further increase our natural levels of mindfulness, we can also deliberately engage more fully with everyday activities. Again the list is endless and can range from the most mundane things like cleaning our teeth and walking to the station, to more complex things like driving and really listening in meetings at work. Again, it is just about engaging our attention fully with whatever is happening in the senses from moment to moment. This heightens the experience of doing whatever we are doing. Sometimes when people find it hard to establish a formal meditation practice, cultivating mindfulness of everyday activities is a great place to start. Having said that, formal meditation is central to really growing the mindful muscle, as the more intensively we practise something, the better we get at it.

Mindful eating simply means to really taste the food, notice its smell and texture and be aware of how we feel as we are eating it. Mindful walking simply requires noticing the sensations of the feet on the ground, the movement of the muscles and the changing centre of balance as we move. And taking a mindful shower involves really tuning in to the pleasant sensations of the warm water, rather than using shower time as an opportunity to worry or plan. We can bring this same basic approach to any activity.

Developing mindful qualities

Mindfulness has a number of central qualities, including attention, awareness, curiosity, gentleness and unconditional friendliness. In any moment where we are truly present, these qualities naturally emerge all by themselves. In contrast, when we are lost in default mode they tend to be absent. The good news is that we can consciously cultivate these qualities, both in our meditation practice and in our day-to-day life.

Attention

Learning to pay attention is the foundation of mindfulness. First we need to recognize what our attention is focused on in any given moment. Then we can start focusing it on what we want it to be focused on — namely, whatever we are directly experiencing through the five senses. As we repeatedly bring it back from default mode to what is right in front of us, we strengthen our attentional control (part of what is known as 'executive functioning'), meaning that we get increasingly better at keeping it focused and recognizing when it has wandered.

Awareness

However, there is a *lot* more to mindfulness than just focusing our attention. As we repeatedly practise mindfulness, we start being less caught up in default mode. We can start simply noticing how thoughts and other distractions come and go. If we look closely, we recognize that there is an awareness that remains even when no thoughts appear. This awareness remains unchanged by whatever is experienced. A metaphor that is sometimes used is that of a mirror, which can reflect anything at all and yet remains fundamentally unchanged — regardless of whether it is reflecting images of heaven or hell.

EXERCISE: CONTACTING AWARENESS

To get directly in touch with what we are talking about here, take a moment to become interested in what it is that is looking through your eyes right now. What is hearing through your ears, what is aware of the sensations in your body? What is thinking the thoughts in your mind?

Don't try to work this out intellectually. Instead, see if you can *experience* it directly. This is sometimes called a 'non-cognitive' inquiry.

This awareness is there all the time — we just don't generally stop to notice it because we get so caught up in the *contents* of the mind. But as we become more and more familiar with awareness itself (by getting less caught up in default mode) we can remain stable even when things are unpleasant and difficult. This is the source of true resilience, and the ultimate goal of mindfulness practice.

Embodiment

One of the most important things that mindfulness practice does is get us back in our bodies. In Chapter 6 we explore intimacy in more depth, where it will become obvious why it is crucial to be in touch with our bodies and able to relate in friendly ways to whatever we experience there. Being able to do this is at the very heart of intimacy, connectedness and true relationship.

However, on an even simpler level, getting in touch with our bodies has a number of extremely beneficial effects. For a start, it gets us out of our heads. While the body and mind are two sides of the same coin we can also think about them as being two ends of a continuum. If we are completely cut off from our body, we very easily get lost in our thoughts. Literally grounding ourselves through embodiment — for instance by practising body scan or breath meditations — means that we don't get so caught up in default mode.

Tuning in to what is happening in our bodies also lets us know what is happening in our emotions, since these have both a cognitive (thinking) and somatic (feeling) component. This awareness allows for early detection of emotional states, giving us more choices about how we respond to them. And when we can bring an attitude of friendly curiosity to the somatic component of an emotional reaction, while letting go of the cognitive component — the 'story' — we become less reactive and better able to tolerate strong emotions. Embodiment also gives us the opportunity to get in touch with pleasant emotions such as joy and bliss (which we miss if we are not able to feel our bodies) and gives us direct feedback, letting us know when we go beyond our limits.[9] As we will see throughout later chapters, these latter benefits are crucial for healthy relationships.

As a note of caution here, people who have experienced trauma sometimes have a difficult relationship with their body. In these cases, it can be advisable to start practising mindfulness by focusing on senses other than touch. There are four others to choose from! And then, once a degree of attentional stability has been achieved, we can start gently sensing our way into our body, being careful not to dissociate or get overwhelmed. Getting in touch with qualities of unconditional friendliness and loving presence first can also be helpful.

Curiosity

One thing that can really help us get in touch with this space of awareness is the quality of curiosity. When we are young we are naturally curious. Just watch little kids putting everything in their mouth or marvelling at the veins on a leaf they have found in the park. But as we get older we lose that innate sense of curiosity and we start relating to the world through concepts and ideas. We start taking things for granted. We lack the freshness of looking at the world with the eyes of children.

The good news is that curiosity is an innate quality. This is why it appears spontaneously in little kids, or even in us when we experience something new. We never actually lose it — we just lose *touch* with it. And of course, this means that we can reconnect with it by deliberately cultivating it. If you want to experiment with this, bring a sense of genuine interest to the breath you are taking right now. Without thinking about it, become curious about *this* breath, noticing it as fully as possible. And realize that you can bring this same quality of curiosity to anything, moment by moment.

Being genuinely curious and interested in this way has the result of deepening our attention. For instance just notice how it helps you engage more fully with the breath. Also, in any moment that we are genuinely curious we can't simultaneously be resisting or judging what we are experiencing — the two are incompatible. So curiosity also deepens our acceptance and non-judgement. You might consider the difference between 'accepting' that a family from another culture has moved in next door and actually being curious about who they are, inviting them into your house and getting to know them.

Non-judgement

Central to mindfulness is also the quality of non-judgement. If the mind wanders it is by definition in default mode. If we then evaluate this mind wandering (by deciding that it is 'good' or 'bad') we are even further into default mode. Instead, we need to practise simply noticing the mind wandering and then just bringing our attention back. With consistent practice, we become naturally less judgemental in everyday life, since anything we practise we get better at. This tends to come as a big relief, given the tension and conflict that judging and evaluating everything tends to create in our lives.

Gentleness

Related to this is the attitude of gentleness. When we recognize that it is simply the nature of the mind to wander, it becomes easier to bring it back when it does rather than getting caught up in self-criticism or being tough on ourselves. Just as we wouldn't train a puppy to stay at our feet by being angry and rough with it, the best way to train our mind to remain present is to gently and patiently bring it back each time it wanders. It is possible to be very persistent and even firm as we do this, while at the same time being very gentle. Eventually, the mind begins to settle and also gets the message that we want it to remain in the present. This is how to do the mental retraining of mindfulness practice.

Self-compassion

Finally, when difficult experiences arise it is important to cultivate self-compassion. This refers to an attitude of unconditional friendliness towards ourselves. The default mode for most people tends is to be self-critical when things get hard. In fact, some of the things we say to ourselves we would never dream of saying to anyone else! While self-criticism and a tough attitude may have a positive intent — for instance, to help us avoid making mistakes or to motivate us to perform better — it causes a number of problems such as avoidance anxiety and depression. Mindfulness helps us to cultivate a friendlier, more compassionate stance towards ourselves. Compassion is an innate quality and is present any time we are in the present moment (rather than being caught up in reactions). And it is also a trainable skill, something we can cultivate through practise.[10] Doing so alters the way our brain perceives suffering and naturally leads to actions to relieve that suffering. This, in turn, leads to improved mental health and better functioning for us, and is something that we will revisit many times throughout this book.[11] Jon Kabat-Zinn, a pioneer in the mindfulness movement, emphasized this a lot in his writing. For instance, his classic book *Full Catastrophe Living* mentions compassion 22 times, kindness eighteen times and loving-kindness seventeen times, although people are only starting to grasp the importance of this in the past few years. Jon Kabat-Zinn even said recently that he could have just as easily called mindfulness heartfulness, and in some ways this term better represents what mindfulness really is.

CHAPTER 3

The science of mindful relationships

In this chapter we outline what happens in the brain when we practise and apply mindfulness with ourselves and those around us. This will provide background for some of the things we explore later in the book. It should also, we hope, provide motivation to start practising and applying mindfulness yourself, to improve your mental health and the quality of your relationships. We realize that this may not be of interest to some readers, and if that is the case for you we suggest that you skip to Chapter 4.

Neuroplasticity: rewiring the brain through mindfulness

We have use-it-or-lose-it brains. The 125 billion neurons constantly rewire their 200 trillion connections in response to what we experience. When we learn or do something for the first time, neurons that were previously unconnected wire together in new neural pathways. And when we do things repeatedly — that is, when we *practise* them — these pathways get stronger and stronger. The neurons move further apart to accommodate the new connections, and that area of the brain literally grows, like a muscle. Of course, this can be either good or bad news depending on the area of the brain being exercised.

Unfortunately, most of the time we are 'practising' default mode. As we explored in the previous chapter, whenever we are not focused and engaged in what we are doing our attention tends to wander off somewhere into the past or future, or gets caught up in reacting to what is happening in the present. The neurons in the default mode networks become activated and the circuits become stronger. It then becomes even more likely we will wander off into default mode in the future.

The prefrontal cortex and executive functioning

Being mindful, however, activates different parts of the brain. One of the most important of these is the prefrontal cortex. Situated behind the forehead, the prefrontal cortex is the CEO of the brain. It is primarily involved in what is called 'executive functioning', the regulation and control of all other mental processes. These include regulating the attention, thinking and reasoning, planning and problem solving.[1] The prefrontal cortex is also involved in managing emotions by regulating the activation in the 'emotional brain', the limbic system. It also helps us inhibit impulses, like eating that third piece of cake.[2]

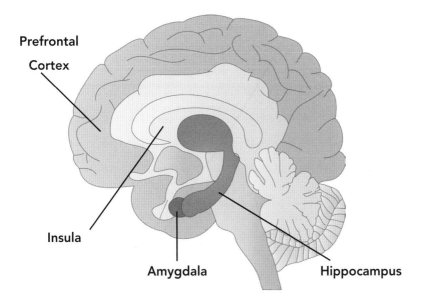

Prefrontal Cortex

Insula

Amygdala

Hippocampus

The prefrontal cortex was the latest part of the brain to evolve. It is more developed in humans than in any other species and is the main reason humans are the dominant species on the planet. It is also the last part of the brain to develop — it does most of its growing between the ages of fifteen and 25. It lets us think of things that aren't actually happening — for instance, imagining the future and remembering the past — giving us a significant survival advantage. However, this ability comes at a cost: the potential to get caught up in worrying about things that may never happen, to ruminate on things that haven't gone to plan and to get caught in judgement and self-criticism. It was because of his prefrontal cortex that Mark Twain said, 'I have had a great many troubles in my life, some of which actually happened.'

The 'fight/flight' circuits

When faced with a genuine physical threat, the amygdala — the 'fear centre' of the brain — becomes activated, triggering the fight/flight/freeze response. This is also sometimes called an 'activation response' as it activates the body for survival, for instance by releasing adrenaline and making us focus on the threat. However, when we are lost in the default mode of worrying and ruminating, we can misperceive things as threats when they really aren't — for instance deadlines, conflict, public speaking and job interviews. The activation response then becomes a 'stress response', which can cause chronic problems for our physical and mental health. We can even suffer what Daniel Goleman calls an 'amygdala hijack', resulting in black-and-white thinking, difficulty planning and staying organized and feelings of panic and guilt.[3] We also tend to feel a sense of separation from others and unworthiness when we are in fight/flight mode, none of which is particularly helpful in relationships.

The stress hormone cortisol is also released. While this can reduce inflammation if we are injured and lays down 'flashbulb' memories of dangerous events so that we can more easily avoid them in the future, chronic cortisol release causes immune suppression and impaired functioning of the hippocampi (which are involved in 'time-stamping' and contextualizing events so we can accurately remember details later).[4] Cortisol also impairs our ability to connect emotionally with others, with obvious implications for our relationships.[5]

Using mindfulness to improve our relationships

Luckily, mindfulness offers a solution. Since attention regulation is a prefrontal activity, bringing our attention back whenever it wanders (without judging or thinking about the mind wandering) forms new connections in the prefrontal cortex. Regular meditation, informal practice and application of mindfulness means we literally build a 'mindful muscle'.[6] And because the amygdala isn't being activated, it starts to shrink (remember, we have use-it-or-lose it brains).[7] Mindfulness gets hardwired in, and default mode gets hardwired out. Also, as the prefrontal cortex is strengthened, we can more easily engage other executive functions like short-term memory, emotion regulation, planning and mental flexibility.[8]

Better executive functioning leads to better health

Because of its effects on brain functioning, mindfulness is effective for treating issues such as anxiety and depression, ADHD and behavioural problems, addiction, eating and sleep issues, personality disturbances and psychosis. It results in increased subjective wellbeing, fewer psychological symptoms, reduced emotional reactivity, and improved behavioural regulation.[9] Mindfulness has also been found to help treat a number of physical problems such as chronic pain and fibromyalgia, headaches and migraines, psoriasis and cytokine levels in certain forms of cancer.[10,11,12,13,14,15] It can even lead to a slowing of the ageing process in our DNA by promoting telomerase activity.[16]

Activating our 'tend-and-befriend' circuits

In direct contrast to amygdala-based fight/flight reactions, the mammalian tend-and-befriend circuits in the brain prompt us to nurture and soothe those around us rather than attack them. They are also the neural basis of empathy and compassion, and are what allows us to have loving, harmonious relationships.[17] Cultivating compassion activates and strengthens our tend-and-befriend circuits.

When we are calm and connected to others we gain the ability to step into their shoes and understand what they may be experiencing. Psychologists call this 'theory of mind', although Daniel Siegel's term 'mindsight' perhaps better captures the essence of what it involves. Mindsight mainly involves the orbitofrontal cortex and the anterior cingulate, brain areas centrally involved in self-awareness and self-regulation.[18] It lets us 'read' the inner emotional state and thoughts of those around us and leads to better relationships. Being present and engaged, noticing cues such as facial expression and the nonverbal components of speech (e.g. tone of voice, rate of speech, prosody), learning the art of 'interoception' (the ability to check in with ourselves and know what we are feeling) and becoming curious about what is happening for other people are all things that we can practise. And anything we practise, we get better at.

Get some insulation: developing loving-kindness and self-compassion

Most people are much harder on themselves than they are on others. This makes sense if we think about it from an evolutionary perspective. For much of human evolution, we have needed fight/flight reactivity to survive. If our ancestors had sat around being loving and gentle they would have been easy prey, so it makes sense that we become reactive when we perceive a threat, even if it's just a look from our partner.

The problem with this, however, is that at the very moment when we are suffering, we amplify this with roughness in a misguided attempt to 'fix' the problem or try to prevent it happening again. But kicking ourselves when life has knocked us down just adds to the problem. Instead, the best thing to do is to soothe ourselves with mindfulness, self-compassion and loving-kindness. The following exercise outlines how to do this.

EXERCISE: GROUNDING AND SOOTHING OURSELVES WITH MINDFULNESS

Take a moment to tune in to yourself. It may help to close your eyes. Take a few mindful breaths and use this to ground yourself. Simply breathe naturally and feel the air entering and leaving the body. Notice the natural expansion and contraction as the body breathes.

Now simply note what is happening for you, right now. How does your body feel? What emotions are around? What is happening in your mind?

See if you can simply allow whatever you are experiencing to be exactly as it is. If there is tension in the body, allow it to be there. If you notice thoughts, let them come and go without trying to do anything with them. If any emotions are around, just name them to yourself (if you can) and let them be there.

Use your body and your breath to stay present, and have the intention to simply create space for whatever is happening in this moment. Give yourself permission to have this experience, just as it is. You might like to place a hand on your heart or wherever you feel the emotion most strongly, directing a sense of unconditional friendliness towards yourself. You can even try offering yourself soothing words like 'This is a totally normal human emotion' or 'I can be with this'.

If you catch yourself reacting, simply notice that and remember that all you are doing here is exploring what happens when you allow everything to be as it is.

Whatever arises, greet it with an attitude of genuine acceptance. Be kind to yourself, perhaps gently acknowledging the emotion or tension and allowing it to be there. Notice what happens when you open to the experience of the present moment, just as it is. While there is no particular experience you should have, and no way to get this exercise 'right' (or wrong), when you genuinely open to things as they are and bring an attitude of friendliness to your experience, you might find that you get in touch with a sense of spaciousness. There is a loving presence that is always there, waiting to be discovered, which is not in resistance to anything that is happening.

As you get more in touch with this loving presence, you will find that you are able to let things be more and more as they are. Keep returning to this throughout the day. Simply keep coming back to the inquiry, 'What happens when I bring an attitude of loving presence to things as they are?'

Research shows that being kind to ourselves and bringing a non-judgemental awareness activates the insula, a brain area centrally involved in self-awareness and interpersonal functioning.[19] Loving-kindness meditation helps cultivate this capacity. Strengthening our insula through mindfulness is one of the foundations of having better relationships. Loving-kindness meditation also reprograms the brain's negativity bias by learning to focus on — and notice — positive experiences. It is an excellent antidote to self-criticism and relationship conflict.

EXERCISE: LOVING-KINDNESS MEDITATION

Get into a comfortable position, sitting or lying. Relax the body and let go of any thoughts of the past or future. Allow the body to settle.

To help us connect to a genuine, heartfelt sense of loving-kindness it can be helpful to first bring to mind someone you love, someone you feel a good connection with. It might be your partner or a family member. It might be a pet or a religious figure. If there are many candidates, well ... lucky you! Just pick one person. Imagine them in front of you. Really sense them being there. Feel the good connection. Notice how this feels in your heart, tuning in to any sensations of warmth or openness. Take a few moments to enjoy this.

Now, staying in touch with this felt sense of goodwill, send some kind wishes your way. Classic wishes are:

- 'May I be happy'
- 'May I be well' (that is, physically and psychologically healthy)
- 'May I be peaceful' (that is, content and okay with yourself just as you are)
- 'May I be safe from harm'.

Keep repeating these wishes to yourself, really connecting with each one. You might like to simplify it by just repeating 'May I be happy'. Alternatively, there might be other wishes you want to make for yourself, such as 'May I be successful ... loving ... healthy ...

May I get that job' etc. Just discover for yourself what rings true and connects you more and more with a genuine sense of kindness for yourself.

Then bring to mind someone you love. It could be the same person you started with or it may be someone else. Just pick one person. If you can, allow the felt sense of goodwill to radiate out from your heart as you make wishes for them: 'May *you* be happy', 'May you be well' etc.

Notice what it feels like to send wishes to this person.

Then bring to mind someone you feel indifferent towards. Actually, this is most people in our lives. Perhaps a neighbour or a shopkeeper, your train driver this morning or the person who sits in the cubicle across from you. Send kind wishes their way: 'May you be happy', 'May you be well' etc.

And now bring to mind someone you have some difficulty with, some conflict with or something unresolved. Don't go for your worst enemy here, for whom it is going to be too difficult to keep your heart open. Maybe just start with someone you have some minor conflict with. Send kind wishes their way. It can help to realize that people who are difficult are just caught up in default mode with little insight into this, and that reacting to their reactions just adds fuel to the fire. It can also be helpful to recognize that these people might make our life hard for five minutes here and there, but they are like this with themselves 24 hours a day! So send them wishes, recognizing that if they were genuinely happy they would be easy to be around. People who are difficult are suffering, and happy people don't cause problems for others. Therefore, even from the level of self-interest it makes sense to wish them well: 'May you be happy', 'May you be well', etc.

Even if it feels mechanical, just send out the wishes. If your heart feels closed, try to open it just a little. Or at least have the intention to open it when you are ready.

Finally, sense all beings everywhere. Perhaps just the people of the Earth, though you may like to include animals and other beings in the oceans, under the ground, off in the farthest reaches of the universe, etc. Include yourself. Sense your connectedness with all of life, and make wishes: 'May *all beings* be happy'.

Allow the felt sense of goodwill to radiate out from your heart as widely as possible.

To finish, take a few moments to sense your body and mind once again. Notice the effect the meditation has had on you, particularly any pleasant feelings. Sending kind wishes and cultivating loving presence releases the hormone oxytocin in the brain and you might feel its pleasant effects, such as feelings of calm and peacefulness. Or perhaps you noticed where you are closed and blocked, where your heart was contracted or too afraid to open. As always, there is no right or wrong. The point of this exercise is just to notice what is true for you, and to cultivate the ability to be kind to yourself and others even when things are difficult.

Sometimes in relationships we can find ourselves experiencing fight/flight and tend-and-befriend activation at the same time, leading to the sense of push/pull that we all experience at times. This is especially likely if we have been hurt. It can be good to give ourselves permission for this to happen and at the same time use mindfulness and loving-kindness practices to calm and soothe ourselves. We explore how to do this in our relationships in later chapters of this book.

PART 2

The mindful self

CHAPTER 4
How to meditate

In Chapters 1 and 2 we saw how mindfulness is our relationship with ourselves and then by extension with the people and things around us. We outlined it as an everyday experience of being present and open, which we all spontaneously experience at times. We also saw how we can practise it when we get caught in default mode, intentionally cultivating qualities of awareness and openheartedness, rewiring our brain in the process. In this section, we explore how to do this.

Why meditate?

A common question that arises when people start learning mindfulness is whether meditation is necessary or whether they can just informally apply mindfulness in their lives, for instance by paying more attention while they eat or work or communicate. The answer is both! People experience significant benefits from simply making an effort to be more present in day-to-day life, and regular meditation makes these benefits even more pronounced. And when learnt in a structured course, their mindfulness increases just because the regular reminders and ongoing conversation about its applications keep it front of mind for them. However, the research shows that it is people who establish a regular meditation practice who continue to benefit the most once the course is over.

A good way to think about it is to think about a game of sport. Imagine you wanted to play soccer well. You wouldn't just run onto the field and hope for the best. Maybe you would manage to finish the game without getting injured, and you might even score a goal if you're lucky. But if you went to a few training sessions beforehand and practised the basic skills you would have a better chance of playing well when you were on the field and in the midst of the game. Another way to put it is that it's best not to wait until you're drowning to learn how to swim. In the same way, practising the skills — or, more accurately, the *way of being* — of mindfulness when you *don't* need them, means that you will be more able to access them when you do.

Meditation helps us systematically retrain the default mode habits of mind wandering, autopilot and reactivity. We get better at recognizing when we have gone into default mode and better at bringing our attention back and re-engaging with what is actually happening. As we explored in Chapter 3, when we practise this repeatedly we form new connections in the prefrontal cortex and literally build a 'mindful muscle'. This muscle then helps us to be mindful throughout the rest of the day.

The other big benefit of meditation is that it creates 'laboratory conditions' for us to explore the nature of our mind. By removing distractions (the extraneous variables) we can start to see what is actually happening in our mind from moment to moment. We start to notice the default mode activity that was there all along but which we didn't previously notice because our minds were so busy. We start observing habits of judgement and reactivity that happen outside of our awareness in our day-to-day life. As we learn about our mind in meditation, we start to notice its functioning throughout the rest of the day. This gives us the opportunity to change what we are doing. With awareness comes *choice*. Without awareness, we just keep unconsciously repeating the same old patterns — and getting the same results. This increased intimacy with our own experience makes it possible to start genuinely becoming intimate with others. Mindfulness meditation begins being about us, but naturally becomes about others and how we relate to them.

How to do it

So how exactly do we do this thing called mindfulness meditation? First up, we recommend that interested readers find some kind of guided meditations to use as training wheels while they begin. There are a growing number of free mindfulness apps such as Smiling Mind and Headspace available that contain different meditation practices of varying lengths. Better still, you might like to find a course that helps you get established in a regular practice and teaches you to apply mindfulness to enhance your wellbeing and/or performance. A quick search online these days is likely to turn up something in your area.

However, if you want to get started right now, here is a basic mindfulness meditation that you can start to practise. Once you have done it a few times and have become familiar with its structure, you can even set a timer and just lead yourself through it.

EXERCISE: BASIC MINDFULNESS MEDITATION

For the next five minutes, sit somewhere comfortable where you won't be too distracted. Perhaps set a timer on your phone. Close your eyes (or just gently let the lids rest in a half-closed position if that's more comfortable). Bring your attention to your body. Notice your posture and ensure you are sitting in a way that embodies alertness and relaxation at the same time. As a starting point, it can be good to make sure the spine is straight. The idea here is to practise 'falling awake' and zoning-*in* rather than zoning out and getting into a dreamy state.

Check in with your body. Notice the state it is in, without judgement or trying to fix anything. If you notice any tension in the muscles, feel free to let that go. We can't force the body to relax but we can let go of tension once we become aware of it.

In the same way, notice any 'mental tension' — default mode activity — and let go of this. By 'let go' we just mean don't focus your attention on it. Instead, simply redirect the attention back to the body and what you can feel there. If the thought subsides by itself, simply notice that. And if it continues, just let it be there without resistance and notice what that is like. In this way, 'letting go' might be better thought of as 'letting be'.

Now bring your attention to your breathing. Trust that your body knows exactly how to breathe and just allow it to do that without trying to manipulate it in any way. Simply notice when you are breathing in and when you are breathing out. Start to notice the pauses between the breaths, which will then let you notice the very beginning of the next breath.

Recognize that it is inevitable that your mind will wander — this is just its nature. Any time you recognize that it has, simply return your attention to the breath. See how gentle and patient you can be as you do this.

Remember: it's not about stopping the mind wandering. It is just about getting better at recognizing when it has. You might even like to be happy when you realize that it has, because this is actually a moment of mindfulness. It is like waking up from a daydream. It really doesn't matter where your attention goes, how long it has been there or how many times it wanders. The practice of mindfulness is simply to recognize when it has and bring it back to the breath. To *this* breath, in *this* moment.

Remember, you can meditate on anything happening in the five senses (touch, vision, hearing, smell and taste). In fact, you can even meditate on thoughts and emotions, although it can be pretty easy to get lost in them. This is why it is generally recommended to start in the five senses, particularly the body.

Establishing a regular meditation practice

Some people find establishing a regular meditation practice easy, but many people struggle. Many people we have spoken to have had a stop–start practice in the beginning, and some people in our courses don't manage to get a formal meditation practice happening at all. However, with commitment, persistence and the right mindset it is possible.

The first thing that helps is simply committing to practice. As with anything, if we don't make the commitment to sit and meditate we are unlikely to do so. Often, people quite quickly begin experiencing the benefits of practice but sometimes it requires a bit of a leap of faith. Just being willing to practise for a week or so and see what happens can be a good jumping-off point.

Another thing that is really helpful is to start small and build confidence slowly. We generally suggest that people start with five minutes of meditation at a time, ideally twice a day. Some programs, such as Mindfulness-Based Stress Reduction (MBSR) and Mindfulness-Based Cognitive Therapy (MBCT) require 45 minutes of meditation a day, and the research suggests that people generally commit to this. But there is not a huge amount of follow-up research showing whether people continue with this long after the programs are over, and our experience tells us that people are much more likely to stick with it if they do a manageable amount. Even just five to ten minutes a day very quickly creates noticeable benefits for most people, such as being calmer, more focused and less reactive — or more aware when they *are* caught up in default mode. It is important to take time to notice these benefits — both during and after meditation sessions — as this provides motivation to continue practising. Once people have established a regular five-minute practice, they can then start gradually increasing it to ten or twenty minutes or even more, depending on what works for them.

A good approach is to treat it as an experiment. There is no 'ideal' time or way to meditate and it is a very individual journey. We suggest people 'bookend' the day with meditation — that is, do it first and last thing. This means they start the day with mindfulness, which makes it more likely they will remain present during the day, and then end the day with meditation so they can let go of physical and mental tension, which tends to improve sleep quality. But if we have little kids at home, meditating first thing is unlikely to work very well. Then the best time might be when we are on the train heading to work or when we turn off the ignition in the car park and before we go inside. Or perhaps at night is going to be a better time.

Here are some tips that we have found work well:

- Start with the intention to meditate at a regular time each day, ideally morning and night, but see what actually works for you.

- Tying your meditation in with an existing routine helps e.g. after showering but before breakfast.

- Meditating as soon as possible after rising in the morning maximizes the likelihood of it happening, as once we get into the routine of the day it is easy to forget or put it off and not get around to it.

- A regular place can be good too e.g. a particular chair in a quiet room.

- It can be helpful to set alarms on your phone or put post-it notes or some other visible reminders around.

- Take a mental note of what *supports* the practice (e.g. set time, set place etc.).

- Conversely, notice what *obstacles* arise — see if you can notice these without judgement, as when we judge things as 'bad' they feel unpleasant and we don't want to look at them long enough to learn from our experiences.

- Notice any benefits, such as relaxation, greater focus or better sleep and use this knowledge to encourage you to maintain your practice.

- Recognize that a sense of things 'getting worse' once you begin to establish a regular practice (e.g. being bombarded by thoughts or becoming aware of unpleasant sensations in the body) can actually be a sign of progress — this can reflect greater *awareness* of things that were already happening but that you hadn't clearly noticed before.

- And realize that it takes time to get a practice going. Be patient.

Mindfulness is tuning *in*, not tuning out

When starting out with a mindfulness practice, it is also important to realize that there is no particular experience you are meant to have. While mindfulness often leads to a sense of heightened wellbeing, at times you might become aware of extremely unpleasant sensations, thoughts and emotions. Many people were originally globally positive about mindfulness and talked about it as if it were some kind of magic potion or panacea, but now (thankfully) the research is becoming more nuanced and people are acknowledging that what we experience when we tune in and get present is not always pleasant. The whole purpose, after all, is to get more in touch with *what is*, and if what is coming up is unpleasant, the experience of sitting with that is likely to be unpleasant. Of course, when we practise bringing a non-judgemental, unconditionally friendly attitude toward whatever is experienced, this tends to mitigate much of the unpleasantness.

Similarly, it is important to be gentle with ourselves when we start meditating. The default setting is to be harsh with ourselves and to try to control our experiences, and this unsurprisingly has a way of finding its way into our meditation practice. Many people start meditating to control their minds, for instance trying to focus on the breath so they don't get caught up in things that are unpleasant. Later on, with sustained practice, this unwinnable control agenda can become obvious, and meditation then changes to an emphasis on being with whatever is experienced without judgement or reaction. Lots of books on mindfulness emphasize this attitude of non-judgement. But even this isn't the full picture, although many people (including mindfulness teachers and therapists) get stuck here. Once we realize that if we sit with our experiences without judgement or resistance they pass, the trap is to start 'sitting with' unpleasant things waiting for them to go away. Of course, this isn't actually acceptance, but a very subtle form of resistance masquerading as acceptance.

What we need to do at this point is to be willing to feel our way back *in* to the unpleasantness of whatever we are experiencing. This is where embodiment, which we discussed in Chapter 2, becomes central. We need to be able to fully feel what is happening in our body, and to practise sitting with it — not so that it goes away (even though it might) but so that we develop a greater capacity to be with it *as it is*. A good metaphor is of creating an ever-expanding container for whatever is happening. Neurologically, the prefrontal cortex (PFC) becomes stronger, especially the insula and medial PFC, and this increases our capacity to regulate the activation of the limbic system — the 'emotion brain'. When we are able to do this, we become able to 'have our emotions rather than them having us' (as happens when the limbic system is activated without prefrontal cortex activation to counterbalance it).

Simply being present and embodied activates the PFC and helps us to genuinely be with what we are experiencing. If we notice an emotional reaction, it can be very useful to name the emotion we are experiencing. This simple act of naming the emotion without judgement further activates the prefrontal cortex, which then reduces the activation in the limbic system.

What also helps hugely is to deliberately cultivate an attitude of unconditional friendliness toward ourselves. As we have already said, the attitude of non-judgement commonly emphasized in the literature on mindfulness is important, but not enough. We need to be able to fully experience what is happening for us with a sense of unconditional friendliness for ourselves as we do so.

Jon Kabat-Zinn calls this 'heartfulness', psychologist and meditation teacher Tara Brach calls this 'radical acceptance' and researcher Kristin Neff calls it 'self-compassion'. Whatever term we use, this is one of the central qualities of mindfulness and one of the most transformative things that we can bring to any relationship — whether that be with ourselves or others.

Once we become able to genuinely be with what is happening, with this attitude of friendliness (some would call it love), we begin *truly* practising mindfulness. Prior to this there is always some subtle control agenda at play. But when we can allow whatever arises to simply be there as it is, we become fully present. We also become incredibly resilient since we cease being so affected by what happens. Although it is important to say here that we never cease *feeling* unpleasant emotions. Again, it can be very tempting to try to use mindfulness to achieve this — or at least to live in hope that one day, if we meditate enough, we will experience this. But we live in a world where discomfort is inevitable. We have bodies that get old and sick and eventually die. Even the most solid-seeming things — seemingly 'perfect' relationships, possessions, even diamonds — are conditioned and eventually break or end. And if we choose to live meaningful lives we will unavoidably experience some discomfort — for instance, if we value interpersonal relationships we will inevitably get disappointed or hurt. But mindfulness helps us to learn to be with this as it is, without feeding it with stories that add fuel to the fire, or fighting it, which creates additional tension. This is the highest meaning of mindfulness. Oh, by the way, if this sounds a little different from your experience of meditation, one thing that may help is to acknowledge that this state of complete, genuine and heartfelt acceptance of everything, just the way it is, is commonly called enlightenment! It is what we can assume the Karmapa or

Dalai Lama experiences. It was also the message of Jesus. It is nice to know what is possible, but can also be useful to acknowledge that most of us are a long way from there. In the meantime, though, as we head in that direction, we experience ever greater levels of awareness and wellbeing.

One of the best ways to establish an ongoing practice is to integrate our meditation with our day-to-day life. That is, to find simple ways of reconnecting with awareness and unconditional friendliness throughout the day, bringing mindfulness to mundane tasks such as work and brushing our teeth, and punctuating the day with short (i.e. five second) meditations. We explore these notions of applied mindfulness and informal practice in detail in the next chapter.

CHAPTER 5
Applying mindfulness

A regular meditation practice is central in that it shows us what is happening in our minds and creates the neurological changes that support us being more aware and unconditionally friendly with ourselves and others. But it is how we *apply* mindfulness in each moment that really makes the difference in our lives. In this chapter we explore a number of common applications of mindfulness and outline how you can start developing being more engaged with your life and more connected to a sense of belonging. These things work together to enhance wellbeing and functioning.

Informal practice

As we said in the last chapter, one of the best ways to establish an ongoing practice is to integrate our formal meditation practice into our existing routine. We can do this by simply being more present while doing everyday tasks such as working, travelling, communicating or doing chores. Life is in fact comprised of a series of tasks and moments, which we can either do mindfully or on autopilot. As we have seen (and no doubt know through our own experience), the former tends to lead to dullness and stress, while the latter tends to produce a sense of aliveness, wellbeing and enhanced performance.

EXERCISE: MINDFULNESS OF EVERYDAY ACTIVITIES

Take a moment to pause and become aware of what you are doing right now. This is not a 'meditation' exercise as such, so there is no need to close your eyes or sit in any particular way. Just tune in to what it is like to read this book. Let go of any thoughts you may have about what you are reading, and notice what it is like to simply let your eyes move over the words on this page and take in the information. If distractions or judgement get in the way, just notice this and come back to reading. You might like to become aware of your body and the contact it is making with whatever is supporting you. Maybe notice your breath. Or the sounds around you. Or you might like to keep your attention engaged with reading.

Now think about what you are going to be doing for the rest of the day. Pick an activity that you might normally do in default mode, such as eating, walking or cleaning your teeth. When you do this activity, have the intention to be fully present while you do it. For instance, if you choose to clean your teeth mindfully, really let yourself taste the minty freshness of the toothpaste and feel the sensations of the toothbrush on your teeth and gums, notice the movement of the muscles in your arm, etc. Be genuinely interested in what it is like to clean your teeth, and notice what effect this has.

The list of informal mindfulness practices is limitless. Here are a few things you might like to experiment with. Just remember to do them with full awareness and curiosity.

- When you first wake up in the morning, before you get out of bed, feel your body. Stretch like you did when you were a kid, remembering how good this feels. Take a few mindful breaths. Connect with your intention for the day ahead. Notice which foot you step out of bed with.

- Find some touch points in your body e.g. feeling your feet on the floor, your breath coming and going or the feeling of your heart beating. Reconnect with these as much as possible during the day.

- Throughout the day, take a few moments to bring your attention to your breathing. Set a timer to remind you to be present.

- Notice the sounds around you throughout the day. Really tune in to the sound of the wind, rain, traffic and birdsong etc. Listen to the background hum of conversation.

- Whenever you eat or drink something, take a moment to really connect with it. Pause and check in with yourself. How hungry are you? What kind of food is your body asking for? Reflect on where what you are about to eat has come from, the fact that it grew somewhere or was made by someone, and wonder for a moment how it got to you. Connect with the sensory experience of eating — with the taste, the smell, the texture. Notice the act of eating — the chewing, the urge to swallow, the actual swallowing. Pause afterwards and tune in to the effect on your body of eating certain foods. Savour the experience.

- Notice your body while you walk or stand. Take a moment to notice your posture. Pay attention to the contact of the ground under your feet. Feel the air on your face, arms and legs as you walk. Are you rushing? Is your mind already where you are going? Come back to each step.

- Bring awareness to listening and talking. Can you listen without agreeing or disagreeing, liking or disliking, or planning what you will say when it is your turn? When talking, can you just say what you need to say without overstating or understating? Can you notice how your mind and body feel?

- Whenever you wait in a line, use this time to notice standing and breathing. Feel the contact of your feet on the floor and how your body feels. Bring attention to the expansion and contraction of your abdomen.

- Be aware of any points of tightness in your body throughout the day. See if you can breathe into them and, as you exhale, let go of excess tension. Is there tension stored anywhere in your body? For example, your neck, shoulders, stomach, jaw or lower back? If possible, stretch or do yoga once a day.

- Focus attention on your daily activities such as brushing your teeth, washing the dishes, brushing your hair, putting on your shoes, doing your job. Bring curiosity and awareness to each activity.

- Before you go to sleep at night, take a few minutes and bring your attention to your breathing. Observe five mindful breaths.

Mindfulness is an everyday experience — of being present and engaged.

When we apply mindfulness in these ways it ceases to be some kind of meditation 'exercise' that we do for ten or twenty minutes a day while we then spend the rest of our waking time in default mode.

Instead, we start punctuating the day with moments of mindfulness and pretty quickly this starts to lead to spontaneous mindful moments, where we suddenly find ourselves being aware, curious and unconditionally friendly without making any effort to do so. In fact, it is crucial that mindfulness becomes something spontaneous and alive, rather than something boring and contrived. It is about rediscovering the freshness and vitality of each moment.

As we keep practising, these moments of spontaneous mindfulness become more and more frequent and we soon start to find that they blend into one another, with the result that we sustain mindfulness for longer and longer periods. According to classical teachings on mindfulness, if we practise enough these moments blend into one another so much that we experience one single mindful moment. The technical term for this is 'enlightenment'. Along the way though (and let's face it, most of us are far from having this experience), we experience more and more moments of genuine wellbeing, where we feel deeply connected to ourselves and the world around us. This sense of connectedness and genuine intimacy with all of life is what mindfulness is really all about.

Reducing stress and managing difficult emotions: letting go of resistance

Stress is so commonplace these days that often we don't even notice it is there. While there are a number of definitions of stress, such as 'demands exceeding resources', we use the term here to refer more to the experience of overwhelm, anxiety, depression and burnout. We do this intentionally, since from a mindfulness perspective stress has much more to do with our *relationship* with what we are experiencing than with the situation itself. Sure, some environments are inherently more 'stressful' than others, for instance being locked in a maximum-security prison versus being on vacation in Fiji. But have you ever noticed how, when faced with the same challenge (e.g. a tight deadline at work) some people get really stressed out and even give up, while others just roll up their sleeves and work to resolve the situation? That's what we are talking about here. Defining stress in this way means that we can use mindfulness to start noticing what is happening in our mind that is causing us stress, and therefore we reduce stress by redirecting our attention to what is actually happening.

To bring this idea to life let's consider the case of Sarah, who came for therapy to help her 'deal better with stress'. Sarah was in her early thirties and had worked for a mid-sized software company for a number of years. Recently, her manager, whom Sarah liked and got along with, had left the company for a larger firm. At once Sarah started clashing with her new boss, Terry. According to Sarah, Terry regularly spoke over her in meetings and she was starting to feel unappreciated and unhappy. To make things worse, the company was being restructured and Sarah suddenly found her workload had significantly increased.

Many people would look at a situation like this and be tempted to conclude that the stress Sarah was feeling was because of the changed conditions at her workplace. Indeed, many of Sarah's friends suggested she should resign and she was starting to seriously consider doing so. However, while it is true that Sarah's job situation had changed in ways that were making her life difficult, it was more empowering to help her recognize the ways that her *relationship* to what was happening were increasing her suffering. What we mean by this is that her tendency to feed her resentment with angry thoughts, or else fight against herself by telling herself that she shouldn't be feeling resentful in the first place (that she was 'being childish' and that this was a '#firstworldproblem'), was what gave rise to her suffering.

You might have heard the expression 'discomfort is inevitable, while suffering is optional'. This is completely true when you look at it. Expressed differently:

Suffering = discomfort x resistance.

What this refers to is the fact that discomfort in life is inevitable. If we choose to live a life where we pursue our passions and values this becomes even more so. For instance, if we value relationships we will inevitably be disappointed. This was part of what was happening for Sarah. She also valued making a contribution, and her sense that this was going unrecognized upset her greatly. But you will notice from the equation above that what is optional (and what increases the suffering) is resistance. The degree to which we resist what is true in each moment is the degree to which we feel stress and suffer. This is what Carl Jung referred to when he said, 'What we resist, persists', and if we come back to how the brain works we see that when we resist something, our attention gets fixed on it (like trying to not think of a pink elephant) and this makes the problem worse.

This 'resistance' can take many forms, the most common being:
- expectations about how things 'should' be
- dwelling on how things once were
- resentment about things not being how we want them to be
- worrying about what might happen
- ruminating and dwelling on what has already happened
- judging and reacting to what we are experiencing.

Sarah was doing pretty much all of these. And this is why she was suffering so much. One of the first things that we tend to do in therapy is to get people to sense into their body and feel what is happening there. This process of embodiment serves two purposes: it gets people out of their heads a little, so that they can start to observe their thoughts rather than being lost in them; and it helps people notice the tension that invariably accompanies resistance to the way things are. Take a moment to try this for yourself.

EXERCISE: NOTICING WHERE YOU ARE RESISTING THE FLOW OF LIFE

Whenever there is tension within the body, this is a sign that we are resisting in some way what is actually happening. Take a moment to pause and check in with yourself. Sense your body and become aware of any areas of tension. Rest your attention there and see if you can notice exactly where the tension is being held. Let it be there exactly as it is. After all, if you try to 'get rid of it' this in itself is resistance and will increase the level of tension. Of course, if it naturally releases once you notice it (which often happens), just notice that.

Now, as a gentle non-cognitive inquiry, simply become curious about what is happening in your mind. Is there a sense of resistance or some judgement about what is happening? Are you reacting to what is happening around you? Are you aware of some body sensation or emotion you don't like? Conversely, are you trying to hold onto something? If there is tension in your body, this process of resistance is *definitely* happening, even if you are not aware of it. Take some time to see if you can notice where the resistance is. Be really curious.

When Sarah started sensing her body, she noticed tension in her shoulders and neck. Tension shows up in different places in different people, but Sarah said that tension in this area of her body was characteristic for her. Therapy then involved getting her to start noticing — as early as possible — when this tension arose at work. As she tuned in to her body in this way, she became increasingly better at catching the earliest signs of tension, and when she then became curious about what was happening in her mind in that moment she began noticing the resentment she had about her old boss leaving, as well as judgements she made throughout the day about Terry's behaviour and a fear that she would have to leave her job, which on reflection she realized she actually really enjoyed. As she became better at catching these reactions, she found that she was less caught up in them. Instead, she became able to calm herself down and focus on what was actually happening. She realized that she had difficulty speaking her mind generally, and that Terry was a perfect mirror to help her to see that more clearly. She also started paying attention to what was happening for Terry, and realized that he seemed insecure and unsure of how he fitted into his new team, given the restructure that was taking place and the resentment of other team members. Sarah found that this realization softened her and she started communicating with Terry in a way that was gentler but also more direct and assertive. Her problems at work started to resolve and she began feeling better about herself generally.

While this is perhaps a rather simple and straightforward situation, it illustrates nicely the way stress gets created in our minds — the 'great many troubles in life, some of which actually happened' that Mark Twain spoke of. This same approach can be used to help reduce any form of distress, including emotions such as anger and severe anxiety. Getting into our bodies is a very important first step.

It gets us out of the extremes of 'feeding or fighting' our emotions. We can start noticing when we get caught up in the story (feeding) or in trying to suppress the emotion or judging ourselves for having it in the first place (fighting) and simply let go of these reactions and bring our attention back to the body. This tends to immediately reduce the associated distress.

We are then left with 'clean emotions' (the raw, underlying emotion) rather than 'dirty emotions' (the secondary emotional reaction that results from an unwillingness to be with the primary emotion). Common primary emotions are sadness, grief and fear. These tend to be accompanied by a sense of vulnerability and helplessness, which most people find it very hard to be with. Instead, we tend to flip to secondary emotions such as anger and resentment (which give us an illusion of control) and anxiety (as we attempt to 'problem solve' our emotions) — or just good old avoidance patterns (including numbing out with substances or food, distracting ourselves with the internet, television or busyness/overwork).

Keep in mind this principle — *don't feed it, don't fight it* — and notice the effect it has on your life.

Getting in touch with and learning to be with primary emotions by becoming more embodied means that we are less driven to distract ourselves. Also, when we 'hang out' with emotions we can start to notice — and resolve — what underlies them. Anger, for instance, is always a cover up. If we look honestly, we will find some vulnerability underneath that we don't feel comfortable being with, which is why we have reverted to anger to protect ourselves.

However, this tends to reflect unmet needs and/or violated boundaries. The emotion itself is therefore a very useful indicator of these things and should not be feared or avoided. Obviously, the expression of anger as aggression or abuse is problematic and should be used with caution. But being willing to feel the anger and then sense that what is underneath it needs attention, is wise and useful. It also helps to name the emotion. As we have mentioned previously, this activates the prefrontal cortex and helps us reduce the intensity of the limbic system activation. This can be difficult at first but becomes easier with practice, as we develop our insula.

Likewise, sensing into sadness, grief or fear and learning to bring an attitude of unconditional friendliness prevents these emotions from turning into depression or anxiety, which commonly happens when we feed or fight them. When we instead sense into the sadness and grief, we usually find something that we need to let go of. This is the wisdom of these emotions. And if we drop beneath anxiety and are willing to contact fear directly, we will find that it is about specific things which we can then address. It is when we refuse to feel our feelings that the energy behind them builds up and becomes rage, depression and anxiety.

We will explore different ways of being with and expressing our vulnerabilities in this way throughout the rest of the book. In general, we can work with emotions at three levels. First, we can use mindfulness to recognize when we are caught up in an emotion, and ground ourselves back in the present through the senses. Second, we can sense our way right to the root of the emotion and address the needs that it is showing us need attention. And third, we can drop beneath even the underlying emotions and make contact with the space of loving presence that is always there. When we do this, emotions can just come and go like the weather, while we remember that we are the sky. When we familiarize ourselves with this and start to trust that we can return to it when we need it, we become able to let go of our defensive strategies and live more in the present.

Using mindfulness to enhance communication

Healthy communication is explored in detail in Chapter 7. Here we briefly explore what it means to communicate mindfully. The default mode of communication is often to speak and listen in distracted ways that are laden with judgement and evaluation. This is especially likely with the people we are most familiar with, such as family members and colleagues.

Using mindfulness to enhance communication is simple. Simply have the intention to really listen to what is being said, rather than waiting for your turn to speak or thinking about something else. Notice if any judgements arise in your mind as you listen, and simply let them be there without feeding or fighting them, bringing your attention back each time to the conversation you are having with the person in front of you (rather than the conversation you might be having in your head). And when you are speaking, notice how laden your speech can be with judgements and assumptions. See if you can set these aside and describe what is actually *true* (for you, at least) in that moment. Communicating mindfully improves the quality of the relationship, results in more effective communication and can even lead to increased empathy and intuition.

Self-care: creating a sustainable, nourishing lifestyle

Using mindfulness to enhance self-care is an enormous topic and we could dedicate an entire book to it. However, here we will briefly explore how increased awareness and loving presence can help improve physical, mental and emotional self-care. We will describe general principles that will help you to notice the effects of your lifestyle choices. When we fully notice the effects our actions have on us, we become genuinely motivated to do the right thing by ourselves.

Most of us live busy lives that are at least sometimes out of balance. The hyperkinetic pace of modern life often means that we pack our days with activity, rushing from one thing to the next. This can become a default setting and we then fail to notice the effects this has on our psyche and our body until we experience exhaustion, dehydration, health problems or burnout. Underlying all of this is the fact that we have lost touch with our bodies and become caught up in activity and thinking. And in amongst all this doing, many of us have forgotten how to simply *be*.

The first step, then, in using mindfulness to improve our self-care is to pause. We can start cultivating the habit of simply stopping momentarily throughout the day, either between tasks or randomly. It is like when we watch a movie and get completely wrapped up in it, but then hit pause on the remote. Suddenly it becomes very apparent that what a moment ago seemed completely real was in fact just a progression of sounds and images on a screen. This pause in the transmission gives us the opportunity to check in with ourselves. We can then start to notice how we are doing. Are we hungry? Thirsty? Tired? What is our mental and emotional state like? What other needs do we have that may need addressing?

And once we notice what we need, we can start to consciously give this to ourselves. And here again, mindfulness helps us to recognize what we *actually* need rather than what we may have been told is good for us. A good example here is eating. From time to time, we see people in our therapy practices with weight issues. While there are often complex emotional and systemic reasons for this, a common underlying trend many times is that they relate to food and eating through concepts and ideas rather than directly experiencing hunger and the effect of different foods on their body. What can be very helpful is to let go of ideas of calories, fat content, whether carbs are good or evil and so forth. Instead, when people start sensing into their bodies they start to notice whether or not they are actually hungry. And if they sit with the question long enough, they can recognize what their body actually needs in any particular moment. Then they can eat using all of their senses, connecting in a deep way with the food they are eating and noticing the effect the type and amount of food has on their body. They can also rediscover savouring, which refers to amplifying the positive experience of eating nourishing, tasty foods simply by focusing on it intentionally for ten seconds or more. When people start eating in this way, many issues with food and weight start to resolve by themselves.

While we have used the example of eating here, this same principle applies to any lifestyle activity. For instance, how much sleep do you need? Some research says eight hours and other studies say six. And then there are those people who sleep four hours a night and run corporations and, in some cases, countries. The answer is that you need as much sleep as you need. And this probably varies at different times. So instead of trying to sleep the 'right' amount, start by tuning in to yourself and noticing if you are energized or fatigued. If the latter, you might want to sleep a little longer tonight than you did last night. And then tomorrow, notice how you feel again. When you trust your body and turn within you start to learn what you actually need. Being attuned to our body in this way has a range of benefits for physical health.

Exercise is another application of this principle. Many people get out of the habit of exercise as they get busier in their lives. Exercising then becomes something they know they 'should' do, which tends to make it an unappealing chore. To counteract this, start very small and take a walk around the block. Walk mindfully and notice how nice it is to simply move (and perhaps connect with the physical environment). Afterwards, take ten seconds to notice and savour how you feel. Focus your attention on the pleasant sensations in your body. These will then be amplified (since, as we have seen, anything we focus on gets hardwired into our brains), in turn motivating you to exercise more.

So far here we have explored physical nourishment but we can extend this to our mental, emotional and spiritual life. When we slow down and check in with ourselves, we have a chance to start recognizing other needs. Perhaps we need to let go of certain thoughts or beliefs that are distressing to us. Perhaps we have been neglecting hobbies or friends. Perhaps we remember that we once had a connection to something bigger than ourselves — whether we call this God or nature or something else — and we might take some time to reconnect with this. We may also start to reconnect with a greater sense of meaning and purpose. Remembering what is important — even simple things like being a good friend or colleague, or contributing to society — can reinvigorate us.

EXERCISE: MINDFUL SELF-CARE

Take a moment to quieten down and sense inside. Notice what is happening in your body and mind. Become interested in what you need right now. Start with the body and its physical needs. Notice whether you feel hungry, thirsty or tired. Don't make any judgements but instead simply note this, with an attitude of love for your body. You may choose to address these needs later, but for now just note their presence.

Now go a bit deeper and notice any emotional or mental needs. Do any emotions need to be acknowledged and allowed to express themselves? Do any thoughts need to be acknowledged? Or let go of?

Then direct this same inquiry to your life more generally. Are there people you have been neglecting? When you tap into this, how does the distance between you actually *feel* in your body? Can you also sense the yearning for closeness with them?

How meaningful do the things you are doing in your life right now seem? What would add even more meaning to your life? Is there anything that you used to do — or have a connection with — that you have lost touch with? See if you can rediscover it in yourself, right now. Hang out with it for a moment and refamiliarize yourself with it.

You might like to make some notes and even commit to putting some of these things into action. But first, really connect with each of these things *experientially*. This is where the real insight (and change) comes from. Resist the urge to skip from one thing to another, instead slowing down and really hanging out with each inquiry, fully experiencing each need.

Martin Seligman began the field of 'positive psychology' by asking the question: 'What are the things that make people happy and lead to flourishing (rather than unhappiness and illness)?' According to Seligman, there are three types of happiness. Gratification results from doing enjoyable things, such as eating nice meals. A stronger, more resilient type of happiness comes from living meaningful lives in accordance with our unique strengths and virtues, what Seligman calls 'signature strengths'. For instance, if we value learning, it will make us happy to read or engage in some form of study, whether formal or informal. More resilient still is being connected to a deeper sense of meaning and purpose. This is what the previous exercise ultimately points you towards. But what goes even further than these three is living fully in the present moment. When we are genuinely here, even simple, everyday things become radiant and vivid. You might think of simple moments when the buzz of default mental activity has fallen away and you have really tasted the food you are eating or connected fully with the person you are talking to or making love to. When we really learn to rest in the present moment, we recognize that it is our mind itself that gets happy, and that this is possible even without enjoyable experiences to trigger this state. If this sounds a little far from where you are right now, don't worry. Just know that if you start to live more in the present moment, you will begin to get glimpses of what we are talking about here.

PART 3

The mindful couple

CHAPTER 6

Intimacy

Love yourself. Then forget it.
Then, love the world.

Mary Oliver

So far in *Mindful Relationships* we have explored how mindfulness helps us become more connected to ourselves, and to learn how to hold what we experience in a space of loving presence. Another name for this is intimacy.

Intimacy is the ability to be in touch with inner experiences — both ours and others'. It is the capacity to directly experience our thoughts and emotions, and to hold these in a space of mindful, loving presence. The origin of the word intimacy is the Latin *intimus*, which means 'innermost' and 'close friend', and most modern definitions refer to a sense of closeness and familiarity. Intimacy, then, begins with developing the capacity to sense into what is happening for us. It is about making friends with ourselves, with what is most true in the depths of our being, and holding this in a loving, gentle way. Following the metaphor of ripples on a pond, once we

71

become intimate with our own inner experience we can start to sense into the inner experience of others, and to remain present and unconditionally friendly toward whatever is happening within them.

In *The Dance of Intimacy*, Harriet Lerner describes intimacy as being able to:

> … *talk openly about things that are important to us, that we take a clear position on where we stand on important emotional issues, and that we clarify the limits of what is acceptable and tolerable to us in a relationship. Allowing the other person to do the same means that we can stay emotionally connected to that other party who thinks, feels and believes differently, without needing to change, convince or fix the other.* [1]

Being intimate in this way is relatively easy when what we are experiencing is pleasant and when the people around us are being agreeable. But when we are feeling vulnerable or there is conflict, the default tendency is to try to avoid or try to control these experiences. Most people find it hard to remain present and loving when vulnerable or faced with unpleasant experiences.

There are countless ways that we cut off from these experiences. The most common is numbing out with drugs and alcohol. Others distract themselves with food, exercise, pornography, the internet and television. Some people busy themselves with work or projects. Still others attempt to control their internal experiences with positive thinking or intellectualizing. And some use blame and anger as ways of directing their attention outward, away from what is hard to be with inside, focusing instead on trying to coerce others or simply being angry at them.

For the most part these 'strategies' are neither good nor bad, in the sense that eating, exercise and moderate alcohol consumption can be quite positive things. But when done to excess they cause problems. Especially when they are done in service of numbing out from, or otherwise avoiding, our vulnerability. When we fall into extremes of feeding or fighting our thoughts and emotions, we set ourselves up for trouble. That is, when we feed the reaction by buying into the story and ruminating, or when we fight against the experience by trying to suppress it, talk ourselves out of it or negate it in some other way, we create problems for ourselves. We end up focusing on it and this perpetuates this issue.

The core issue with many of the clients we see in our clinical practices is exactly this. There is some core wound or vulnerability that they don't want to — or don't know how to — allow themselves to feel, and they are caught up in avoidance patterns. These avoidance patterns — whether they be addiction, overwork and burnout, the anxiety that comes with trying to control and predict everything, or some other strategy — become the presenting issue that brings them to therapy in the first place. Indeed, symptoms are generally attempted solutions to other problems. In relationship counselling, we see the same thing: people cut off from their own internal world, lacking intimacy with themselves and therefore incapable of having intimacy with someone else. If we are unaware of what is happening inside us, or unable to remain present and loving when we are, how can we possibly hope to be aware of, and loving toward what is happening in our partner? It's just not possible.

The path of healing is to sense our way back into what is being avoided, first in ourselves and then in our relationships. Embodiment is the key to intimacy. If we stay in our heads we can never truly develop intimacy with ourselves or others. We need to find ways of experiencing our own and our partner's wounds and vulnerabilities directly and fully, yet without being overwhelmed. And we need to bring an attitude of unconditional friendliness (self-compassion) to our innermost wounds and vulnerabilities. When we are able to do this our symptoms and relationship issues — which, remember, are caused by the very attempt to avoid our vulnerability — tend to resolve by themselves.

Loving presence

To do this, we must develop a container of loving presence that is able to hold whatever is experienced without being overwhelmed. Indeed, the fear of being overwhelmed by emotion and somehow annihilated or becoming unable to function, is the reason we develop avoidance strategies in the first place. Getting in touch with something bigger is critical to the healing process. Mindfulness teacher Thich Nhat Hanh says that it is not enough to just suffer — we must also get in touch with something that can contain that suffering. Mindfulness helps us to contact and relax into a sense of something larger, which brings peace. Therefore, another way to think about mindfulness is holding whatever is true in a space of loving presence. A useful metaphor here is to think of the vulnerability or emotion as a drop of ink. If we put it in a shot glass of water, the ink will completely colour the water. But if we put the ink in a lake or ocean it will be a very different experience. Mindfulness creates this space, which can hold any experience without being changed by it. And when we start to hold vulnerable parts of ourselves in this space, it becomes important that the water is clean and warm. This is the basis of loving presence.

To illustrate this process, let's meet Jane and Michael. Both in their twenties, Jane and Michael presented for couple's counselling, with Jane complaining that Michael worked too much (he was a junior lawyer in a major firm) and was hardly ever home. She felt isolated staying at home every day with their two-year-old son Harry, and she complained that even when Michael was home he was emotionally unavailable and absent. Michael complained that Jane was needy and that he didn't understand what she meant by 'unavailable'. He said he recognized that she felt isolated and made a significant effort to spend time with her when he was home on the weekend. He listed a range of activities they did together, such as going out for meals, taking Harry to the park and watching movies together after Harry had gone to sleep.

Does this situation sound familiar? Perhaps you have experienced it in one of your relationships? Or seen it in someone else? What became immediately apparent, even just watching the way Jane and Michael interacted in the therapy room, was how cut off they actually were from each other. This was obvious even in the subtleties of their body language. Michael thought just spending time with Jane was being intimate, but they were cut off from each other's emotions. This led them to feeling isolated and resentful. And what became obvious throughout therapy was how cut off they were from themselves.

The path to healing their relationship began with healing themselves. Once they were able to acknowledge how afraid they were of being vulnerable, they were able to start letting go of some of their defences. They learnt to soften into deeper, more authentic parts of themselves — what Buddhist teacher Pema Chödron calls our 'tender soft spot' — and to hold these parts of themselves in a space of loving presence. As they did this, they calmed down and became able to see themselves more clearly. Emotions that had been stuck began to move again. They each recognized their fears and unmet needs and found words to express these directly. And as they saw themselves more clearly, they started to see each other more clearly. Both became aware, for the first time in their relationship, that their partner was a unique being, with their own vulnerabilities and insecurities. They sensed each other's tenderness and innocence, rather than getting caught up in projections and defensiveness. And as a result, the way they related to each other changed fundamentally. Jane recognized Michael's need for space to unwind after a stressful day at work. She started giving him time after he got home so he could relax, rather than placing further demands on him. This required that she soothe her own feelings of loneliness and reactive sense of rejection when Michael wasn't immediately available for her upon walking in the door. In return, Michael found that he started to want to spend time with her and Harry. As he got more in touch with his own tenderness — and less afraid of it — he found he enjoyed the feeling of closeness he experienced with his wife and son. The activities they did together took on a new flavour for both of them, as both genuinely connected with each other.

> **We must first cultivate intimacy with ourselves before we can be truly intimate with others.**

EXERCISE: CONTACTING LOVING PRESENCE

You will notice from the title of this exercise that it is more about *contacting* loving presence than cultivating it. Take a moment right now to pause and get present. Centre yourself in your body and become aware of your breathing.

Now drop into that space of presence a simple question: 'Is it not true that loving presence is *already here*, right now, in this moment?' Allow yourself to get in touch with the part of you that can allow everything to be as it is. Relax into this experience and allow yourself to enjoy it.

If you have trouble sensing it, this is just a sign that you are not used to touching it. Many of us are so busy trying to predict and control everything in our lives that we never take time to sense the part of us that can allow everything to simply be as it is.

If this is the case for you, try the following. Bring to mind someone who you feel loving towards and/or feel loved by. Most relationships are complex and you might have mixed feelings, but focus on the love and the sense of being supported. Really sense this person being in front of you. Picture their face. Sense your heart area and allow any warm, pleasant feelings to expand. Allow this sense of goodwill and love to radiate out to this person. And allow it to radiate back from them, right back into your heart. You might like to place your hand on your heart and sense into this loving presence.

Gradually allow this sense of loving presence to expand and infuse your whole being. Breathe with it and let yourself enjoy it fully. After a while, let go of needing to sense the person in front of you and just rest with the feeling of loving presence. You might like to place your hands over your heart and feel the warmth and sense of presence this brings. And it might help to repeat kind wishes to yourself such as 'May I be happy', 'May I be free from suffering' or 'May all beings be happy/free from suffering'.

After you have enjoyed this for a while, let go of any words or images. In fact, let go of any intention at all. Simply rest in loving presence.

Notice what it is like to rest in your natural state.

Learning to love ourselves

We have deliberately been using the term 'ourselves' throughout the book so far. While perhaps grammatically incorrect, the word speaks to a very important point. Our personalities are comprised of multiple parts. At its most basic, we might recognize in ourselves a part that wants to be active and healthy, and another that would quite happily stay on the couch eating ice-cream. Anyone who has quit smoking will know what it is like to have one part that genuinely wants to stop and another that doesn't. In fact, we all have many parts — some loud and expressive and others quiet and receptive. Recognizing this simple truth can immediately help us make sense of how our personalities can seem to change over time, depending on how we feel, where we are and who we are with. It also sheds light on how we can at times experience a very real sense of internal conflict, with two parts pulling us in different directions.

To end this war we need to make friends with, and find a place for, all parts of ourselves. First, we need to be able to recognize the different parts when they show up. All of us identify with certain parts of our personality — for instance, parts that are intelligent, charismatic, productive, witty, etc. And we reject other parts — particularly parts that we see as 'negative', such as angry, sad, insecure, vulnerable parts. The family we were raised in and the culture we live in, as well as our own predisposition and life experiences, influence which parts we see as acceptable and which ones we disown or project onto others. To recognize different parts when they show up it helps to be able to *feel* them. Different parts tend to feel different in our body. Reflect, for instance, on how you feel when you are being productive and energetic and how you feel when you are feeling vulnerable or afraid. As we explored in Chapter 2, being embodied and aware of our physical sensations helps us notice reactivity early, before it takes hold of us. Being aware of our physical sensations also lets us know which part (or parts) of our personality is present. This prevents any one part from running the show unconsciously, which is what causes problems. For instance, if we have a part that likes recognition and is therefore very high achieving, this can be used skilfully for great benefit. But if it runs the show and we don't realize this is happening, we can burn out.

Being able to know which parts are around, and relating to each with an attitude of genuine acceptance and loving presence, means that we cease the internal battle. We make space for all parts of ourselves and start to feel integrated and whole. And when we sense different parts of our personality without judgement or reaction we come to know them fully. We start to see that all parts want something good for us, even if they go about trying to get it in ways that don't work or cause us problems. For instance, many of us contain parts that are fearful of getting hurt. These parts might avoid relationships and can sabotage things or make us run if we start getting too close to someone. This is what was playing out for Jane and Michael. But when we really hang out with these parts, we can see they are trying to protect us from pain. As we acknowledge this and give those parts a place, they settle down. They will still alert us when we are getting close to someone — or conversely, when some issue in the relationship has caused a loss of intimacy — but we can then soothe the fearful part with loving-kindness. We can also take note of the wisdom it is offering.

This last point is important. As we have explored, the default setting for most people is to be afraid of their vulnerability and unpleasant emotions, and to deny, hide or try to get rid of them. But this causes a loss of intimacy, an internal battle, and we also lose the opportunity to recognize what the emotion is telling us. Take anger, for instance. Many people are afraid of anger and judge it as 'bad'. They try to hide it and reject this part of themselves when it shows up (which, ironically, is getting angry at the angry part, if we look deeply). But anger has incredible wisdom. Of course, we need to differentiate it from aggression which, except in rare instances such as protecting ourselves or others from genuine physical harm, tends to cause problems. But the *emotion* of anger is very wise. It shows us that certain needs aren't being met or boundaries are being violated. And when we are able to sit with it and welcome it as a wise part of ourselves, we have an opportunity to actually inquire into what these needs and boundaries are.

We can do this with all emotions and all parts of our personality. Sensing deeply into ourselves and holding all parts in loving presence is an ongoing practice but one that is profoundly healing. In fact, the word 'healing' shares the same linguistic roots as 'holistic' and 'wholeness'. So healing, in the true sense of the word, means to be whole. This requires being intimate with all parts of ourselves, on the deepest level. The internal battle subsides and we start to experience genuine intimacy with ourselves, experiencing a sense of solidity. This is what makes mindfulness such a profoundly healing process. Eventually, we become able to hold our partner's parts in a space of loving presence and experience the joys of true intimacy with another.

The thirteenth-century poet Rumi sums up this process perfectly in his poem *The Guest House*:

This being human is a guest house.
Every morning a new arrival.
A joy, a depression, a meanness,
some momentary awareness comes
as an unexpected visitor.
Welcome and entertain them all!
Even if they are a crowd of sorrows,
who violently sweep your house
empty of its furniture,
still, treat each guest honourably.
He may be clearing you out
for some new delight.
The dark thought, the shame, the malice.
meet them at the door laughing and invite them in.
Be grateful for whatever comes.
because each has been sent
as a guide from beyond.

Our relationship with ourselves *is* our relationship with others

In the next chapter we explore in more detail how we can use mindfulness to enhance intimacy with ourselves and others. But to finish this chapter, we want to explore an important point: the way we relate to ourselves is the way we relate to others. If we are cut off from or rejecting of certain parts of ourself, we tend to do this to others also. Often we don't even realize we are doing this to ourselves, let alone our loved ones. Just like Jane and Michael, we only experience the result — the lack of intimacy and the conflict that goes with it. Once we realize this truth we can start to heal our relationship with ourselves. Intimacy is about becoming more ourselves rather than trying to change ourselves fundamentally in any way. Our true nature — the loving presence that we can contact through mindfulness — is perfect as it is. We just need to identify with this instead of our default mode reactivity. Mindfulness, loving-kindness and self-compassion all help immensely. So too does a genuine desire to welcome all parts of ourself in loving presence. When we can do this with ourselves, it naturally starts extending out to others in ever-expanding ripples.

> **Mindfulness, loving-kindness and self-compassion are powerful tools for cultivating intimacy.**

EXERCISE: LOVING OURSELVES AND OTHERS

This is an extension of the 'Contacting loving presence' exercise on page 76. Take a few moments to relax into (or cultivate, if need be) a sense of loving presence. See if you can get in touch with a part of yourself that is not in opposition to any part of reality. Notice what it is like to simply allow everything to be as it is.

Now, notice how your body is feeling. Simply notice any sensations and allow them to be there. If you notice any tension just allow that to be there too. Go in a bit deeper and sense any emotions that are around, and again simply notice whatever is there.

Then, sense into what part or parts of you are present right now. Do you notice an energetic, enthusiastic part filled with a desire to go out and do things? Or a tired part that needs some rest and nurturing? Do you feel afraid or vulnerable? Ashamed? Irritated or angry? You might like to place your hand on your heart in a gesture of loving presence and simply be with whatever is there.

Simply sense into whatever parts are present right now. Allow space for each of them to be there, just as they are. Welcome all parts of yourself. Notice the feeling of wholeness and healing that emerges when you do this.

If you can't clearly sense any parts at all, that's fine. Just rest in loving presence and gently invite any parts that are present to show themselves. In every moment one or more of our parts are present, but if we have neglected to listen to them they can be hard to notice.

Now, bring to mind someone you are close to. Allow this sense of loving presence to radiate out towards them. Hold them in a space of genuine acceptance and love. Notice what that feels like. If you get caught up in anything else, just come back to loving presence.

And then start to sense what part/s may be present right now for this person. Even if they aren't nearby, you might find you can start picking up on them and get a sense of what is present in them. Again, if you can't sense this just rest in a space of loving presence for them and yourself.

You might like to practise this exercise often during the day, until you become familiar with it. It can also be a wonderful exercise to do *with* your partner or other loved ones, perhaps sitting across from them as you sense into them. You can even open your eyes and gaze into theirs, which tends to deepen the experience even more.

CHAPTER 7
Healthy relationships

*Love and intimacy — our ability to connect with ourselves and others, is at
the root of what makes us sick and what makes us well, what causes sadness
and what brings happiness, what makes us suffer and what leads to healing.
If a new drug had the same impact, virtually every doctor in the country
would be recommending it for his or her patients. It would be malpractice
not to prescribe it.*

These words by Dean Ornish, one of the world's most renowned
experts in mind–body medicine, point to how central relationships
are to healthy lives. However, the quality of the relationship is
crucial. In this chapter we explore what makes for healthy, life-
sustaining relationships — and how mindfulness can help create and
enhance these.

Learning to take another's needs into account while
simultaneously looking after our own is a key difference between
healthy and unhealthy relationships. When we are able to do this
in intimate relationships, a genuine mutuality is fostered. No one
needs to win, and useless battles about power and control tend to be

less prevalent. When we learn to identify and bring loving presence to the vulnerable parts of ourselves as well as the vulnerable parts in our partner, and hold space for both, we can then see what arises. We let go of expectations that things must look a certain way and instead bring acceptance to what is actually occurring. Harville and Helen Hendrix, the creators of Imago couple's therapy and authors of *Getting the Love You Want*, say, 'When we gather the courage to search for the truth of our being and the truth of our partner's being, we begin a journey of healing.'

Relationships fail for many reasons. But generally there are long-term patterns of communication difficulties and conflict, as well as a lack of intimacy. We all bring to our intimate relationships our own history and predisposition to manage conflict in certain ways. We have patterns and styles of communication that might have kept us safe as children but which no longer work as adults. We have fundamental needs that we might find hard to even articulate. Our needs for intimacy vary and this can give rise to problems if not navigated with awareness. Even where there is not a mismatch of needs and *both* parties want deeper connection, often they do not know how to achieve this. Sometimes partners do not even know that this is the problem — they just experience the resulting conflict with no real idea of what is causing it. They come to see the problem as being about the conflict itself, or fixate on certain behaviours they don't like.

Bids for contact

It helps to recognize that the underlying problem here is the unmet yearning for intimacy and closeness. Partners reach out to each other but they miss the cues. Relationship expert John Gottman calls these 'bids for contact'. Partners regularly make these bids, reaching out for contact and intimacy. This can take the form of affirming positive behaviours our partner has made, asking to spend quality time together, physically touching them, giving gifts and doing nice things for them. These bids happen all throughout the day and can be quite subtle. When things are going well, they are noticed and met with a mutual bid or acceptance from our partner. This sets up a positive feedback loop and intimacy deepens.

However, at times we can be so caught up in our own reactivity that we fail to notice the bids or are unable to respond positively. This can happen when we are angry with our partner for something they have done (or not done) or caught up in some story about the relationship. It can also happen when either partner is stressed. Both Jane and Michael (the couple we met in the previous chapter) were making such bids — each in their own way and on their own terms — but these were being missed because of resentment and reactivity. As they developed increased intimacy with themselves, each of them began to be present enough to start noticing the other's bids, which resulted in a strengthening of the relationship and a deepening of intimacy.

Past relationship traumas also leave wounds that make people fearful of showing their vulnerable parts to their partner. When bids are made that deepen the level of intimacy in the relationship, this can be experienced as threatening and leads to defensive, hostile responses or withdrawal. Often this then results in a similar reaction from the person who made the bid for closeness, resulting in a negative cycle of defensiveness, criticism, attack, stonewalling and/ or withdrawal.

Mindfulness is vital in these situations. As we explored in Chapter 2, any time we recognize a default mode reaction we are no longer fully in this reaction. Our partner may be completely amygdala hijacked with little or no awareness this is even happening, but if we remain present, at the very least we don't exacerbate the situation by reacting ourselves. And just as bringing mindfulness and loving presence to our own reactivity helps us soothe ourselves, we can learn to do this for our partner. Learning to respond to our partner's reactivity with loving presence is the basis of interpersonal mindfulness and the foundation of good relationships. We become able to notice and respond to our partner's bids for contact, and enter into a positive feedback loop.

EXERCISE: BRINGING A FRIENDLY PRESENCE TO YOURSELF AND OTHERS

Take a moment to notice what you are feeling. Sense into your body and check to see if you can feel your arms and legs, and feel your feet on the ground. Notice your breath and become aware of any tension or tightness being held anywhere in your body. See if you can just let your breath go there and notice what happens as you breathe into the tension. Whatever you experience in your body and mind, greet it with a sense of genuine acceptance and friendliness. You might imagine how you would relate to a small child who was upset, or an injured animal. Bring this same kindness to yourself.

Once you have relaxed into being with yourself in this way, broaden your awareness to include others. If there are people around you, sense them and allow this attitude of loving presence to radiate out to them. Allow your face to relax and let yourself smile. Notice if this results in an increased capacity for presence and a greater sense of openness to those around you. Simply being mindful enough to smile sends messages of friendliness to others and signals that we are not a threat to them.

If you are alone, just bring to mind people you are close to and hold them in a space of loving presence.

Notice the effect of this exercise on you. Do you feel relaxed or expansive? Or perhaps you have noticed ways you are closed or blocked? What happens when you bring loving presence to this?

Notice, too, the effect this practice has on the quality of interactions with those around you.

Being willing to look deeply

We discussed in the previous chapter our tendency to reject or disown certain parts of our personality. When we reject parts of ourselves these become hidden from us and become what Jung would call the 'shadow' aspect of our personality. This process begins in childhood, when more instinctual, primitive parts of our personality (e.g. sexual desire, hatred, murderous rage, desire for revenge) are superseded by the conscious mind. These then operate outside of conscious awareness and cause problems in our intimate relationships. Often what we react to most in our partner are the disowned parts of ourselves — a process sometimes called 'projection'. When we are caught up in projection we are unable to see our partner clearly, as a whole person. As a result, we are cut off from seeing the good in them and miss or respond negatively to their bids for contact.

Mindfulness helps us look deeply into ourselves. When we become intimate with ourselves we begin to notice the disowned, shadow parts of our personality. We can acknowledge and own our human vulnerability, history and baggage and hold this with loving-kindness. We learn to look below the surface to see what our (and our partner's) reactions actually represent. It's rarely about the toothpaste lid or the socks on the floor! We become able to sit with difficulties and differences of opinion rather than reacting to them or pretending they don't exist. This is a respectful way to be in a relationship.

Mindfulness allows us to respond rather than react to the current situation. When we remain attentive to what is going on for us, we become more aware of what we are thinking and feeling. This allows us to choose how we respond, rather than blindly reacting according to previous conditioning. We activate our tend-and-befriend circuits and our fight/flight reactivity starts to subside.

Our bodies are central in this process. As we saw in Chapter 2, they anchor us in the present and give us a wealth of information. When we allow whatever is happening to simply be there, without judgement or resistance, something very interesting happens. We stop resisting reality and we notice it changes all by itself! When we sense into ourselves in this curious and mindful way, we create space. We feel a sense of relaxation as our body no longer feels under threat and we are able to include our own experience and that of another. This unconditionally friendly attitude leads to compassion and understanding both for ourselves and also for the way our loved ones are experiencing their particular version of reality. We breathe into our feelings and make space for them simply as they are. Then we do it again and again and we begin to make sense of how they came to be, of both of our histories and stories and the impact they have had on us.

Over time, this practice of sensing inwards and moving towards what we are experiencing with an attitude of friendly curiosity allows us to develop our capacity for choice in our relationships. We can choose to sit with difficult feelings and look deeply to see where they come from, rather than reactively trying to 'fix' them. This gives us greater choice about when — and if — we discuss things with our partners. We develop the capacity to tolerate separation and closeness because we no longer avoid and flee from our feelings or those of another. Instead, we are able to acknowledge that it is okay both for us to feel what we feel and for our partner to do the same. We can express and feel a whole range of emotions. We can allow ourselves to be disappointed, sad, angry, jealous or afraid, as well as calm, happy, excited, grateful or energized. And it is okay for our partners to also have their feelings. We know what it is like to be fully alive and fully human as we breathe into an ever-developing sense of self.

> **Our relationship with ourselves is the same as our relationship with others.**

Mindfulness also helps us notice *what* we are reacting to in our partner. Through noticing our reactions, we start to recognize our projection and become familiar with the disowned parts of our personality. We start to notice when they are present and they cease unconsciously driving our behaviour. Jane and Michael achieved this once they stopped blaming each other and became willing to look deeply into their own vulnerabilities and to take responsibility for their own reactivity. This is the true meaning of 'Know thyself', which the Greek philosopher Socrates believed was fundamental to functioning effectively in the world. And when we hold these parts in a space of loving presence, our internal conflict and tendency to project decreases, and we start to feel more integrated. We experience a growing sense of calm in our relationships.

Forgiving others for ways they have hurt us also needs to happen in our body. It is one thing to have the thought that we forgive them and another thing entirely to be able to fully feel the hurt and yet remain connected to a genuine sense of compassion and loving presence. This is true, heartfelt forgiveness.

Communicating effectively

In the beginning of most relationships both partners tend to discuss easy topics that they both agree on as they develop rapport and connection. The 'honeymoon period' tends to wear off, though, as partners are not only focused on the similarities and the idealized version of each other but start to notice and have to manage the differences. As the relationship progresses, they stop discussing the positive things and start noticing and reacting to the points of disagreement. It also becomes increasingly difficult to 'agree to disagree' about things, such as how many children they will want or how much sex they have. As these difficulties arise, it can become difficult to know when and how to talk about them.

This was what was happening for Tim and Amanda, a couple in their late fifties who presented for couple's counselling. With their two children having left the home, they were suddenly unable to focus on their kids and were left to face their obvious differences. They hadn't actually talked about anything meaningful (other than their children) in decades and came to therapy wondering if they should split as they 'no longer had anything in common' as Amanda put it. Actually, as they described the problems they were having it became clear that they no longer had anything *superficial* to discuss, and both tended to avoid talking about the real issues, such as how often they had sex, as they invariably got into arguments when they did. Instead, each held back from saying what was truly important, convincing themselves that it wasn't really an issue anyway. But both were consumed with resentment and tended to blame the other.

This is a common pattern in couples and often leads to divorce. To save the relationship, Tim and Amanda had to be brave enough to start saying what was actually on their minds. Faced with this choice, some couples choose to separate as it can be extremely confronting to speak our truth. But in the case of Tim and Amanda they decided the relationship was worth working for and both signed up for the task of learning how to communicate effectively.

It is important to do this in a way where we express our vulnerability rather than blaming our partner or making them wrong. Timing is also important. A common complaint we hear in our therapy practices is of a partner wanting to discuss difficult issues late at night or when the other person is stressed or tired. Tim and Amanda had suffered from this previously and it was one of the reasons they had closed down and ceased even trying to talk about important issues. It can help to have an agreement about when is a good time, or to request a discussion with a brief 'heads up' about what the concern is and an agreement to discuss it later. It can be good to have an agreement ahead of time that it is okay to defer difficult discussions to a later, more suitable time. However, it is important that an alternative time is specified so the person requesting a discussion is not left hanging or feeling stonewalled. In this way both people care for the relationship. There is a commitment to discuss important matters and not to sweep things under the carpet, but to do so in a manner and time when both can be fully present. Tim and Amanda agreed to this, and it immediately made it easier for them to start communicating more effectively.

It is also important to endeavour to drop beneath reactivity and defensiveness and speak from a place of vulnerability. When we are defensive or attacking, this tends to engender defensiveness and counterattacks in others. Instead, when we learn to express our needs more directly they are more likely to be met. To communicate effectively, we need to be connected to love for ourselves and our partner. Rather than trying to make the other person wrong, we need to just do the best we can and forgive ourselves over and over for our humanness. This requires us to be connected to our bodies, in touch with a sense of caring about our partner as well as ourselves. Then we can directly express our needs rather than talking about what our partner is doing 'wrong'. Demanding our partner change leads to defensiveness, whereas describing our experience in a non-blaming way makes it much more likely we will get what we need. Learning to do this is exactly what helped Tim and Amanda (as well as Jane and Michael from Chapter 4) start communicating clearly. Naming our feelings and acknowledging that we are being triggered stops us from going to the default mode of reactivity. It activates the prefrontal cortex as we in effect press pause and sense inwards, and reduces our tendency to move to blame and project the discomfort outside of ourselves. We instead start to speak our truth.

An important distinction to make here is between experiencing an emotion and acting it out. For instance, when feeling angry we can start recognizing angry reactions as they occur rather than letting anger become aggressive. We can then let our partner know that we are reacting and take responsibility for calming ourselves down. Perhaps our partner can hold space and help soothe us, or perhaps we will need to do it for ourselves. If we can't stay in contact with our partner and use mindfulness to cultivate a sense of mental space, we might even need to negotiate taking some physical space until we can calm down. The important thing to do here is to have an agreement that we will return once we are calm and address whatever triggered us. Returning to resolve the issue prevents a pattern of avoidance being set up. Taking space allows us to acknowledge our own reactivity and to sense into how to express ourselves from a place of presence.

When we take responsibility for our emotions and learn to stay mindful while experiencing them, our emotions actually become a source of wisdom. Many people are at first surprised to hear that their anger is an extremely intelligent emotion. But if we remove judgement about an emotion like anger, we can start to see that it is often a sign that a need is not being met or a boundary has been violated. Frustration and irritation then become valuable friends, pointing us toward deeper truths that need addressing. For instance, we may have difficulty being with an underlying emotion such as sadness, so instead we cover over our vulnerability with anger. Once we have recognized that we are doing this, we can pause when we feel an emotion arising and become curious about what information this is giving us rather than feeding or fighting the secondary emotion. Perhaps take a moment to reflect on this for yourself and you will see that it is true. Having realized this, we can ask directly for needs to be met or boundaries to be respected rather than just saying that we are angry — or worse, acting it out. This makes it more likely our partner will hear this as a request rather than an attack, and we are then more likely to get what we actually need (rather than just more defensiveness).

Learning to sit with and tolerate our own difficult emotions also means we stay more present, which enhances our capacity to read emotional cues from our partner. It helps us to focus on the truth of what we are feeling and not get caught up in the stories we tell ourselves about our partner, as Jane and Michael were doing when they first came for therapy. Mindfulness lets us tolerate our feelings — and even welcome them — so we can then be curious about what they might be alerting us to. It also helps us notice when we are being reactive, defensive, critical or attacking, and to simply acknowledge these reactions rather than feeding or fighting them. Doing both of these things lets us access our feelings more fully and deepens intimacy.

EXERCISE: SPEAKING FROM THE HEART

Sit with your partner and take a few moments to both connect with each other. Open to a space of loving presence.

Now, decide which of you will speak first. If you are the speaker, first pause and sense your heart. What does your heart most want to say to your partner? Allow this to be a gentle inquiry and let the answer emerge in its own time. When words come, speak them as clearly as you can. Then pause and notice what it feels like to have spoken them. See if you can sense their effect on your partner.

If no words come, simply sit in silence, sensing your heart. Words will arise in their own time.

The listener's role is simply to stay present and receive the words. Don't offer advice or feedback.

After a few minutes, when it feels right, swap roles.

Differentiation

While good communication is central to healthy relationships, it is not sufficient on its own. Many relationship therapists work only at this level and then wonder why their clients remain stuck. Instead, it is crucial to learn to recognize and honour our own needs while simultaneously taking our partner's needs into account. Relationship expert David Schnarch refers to this as 'differentiation'. It involves learning to hold onto ourselves while in close proximity to someone we care about, avoiding the extremes of withdrawing or giving in (often resentfully) and losing integrity with ourselves. It means recognizing and then soothing ourselves when our partner's feelings provoke anxiety in us. It means knowing that even if the relationship is going through difficulties we can manage to hold onto our own emotions and not be overwhelmed by anxiety in the face of our partner's (sometimes difficult) emotions. One of the most difficult challenges we go through in relationships is holding onto our own experience and validating that for ourselves even when our partner might not offer this validation and might be even dismissive or put us down.

Clients we see talk about feeling 'smothered' or as if they are 'drowning' in the relationship when they cannot manage to hold onto a separate sense of themselves while staying connected to an intimate other who might also be experiencing distress. They then blame the other for this. They may have to pull away in order to have a sense of self, or pretend and hide what they really feel, thus losing integrity with themselves. Or they might blame or criticize their partner for having difficult emotions, and this can manifest as, for example, anger when a partner is depressed and unavailable. It is as if they cannot see that their partner is a unique individual going through their own particular experience and so cannot hold onto their own separate emotions in the face of this.

Schnarch says differentiating is one of the most important — and difficult — developmental tasks we ever go through, and our experience as therapists confirms this. Many people come to therapy because they have been unable to achieve differentiation. Over time this lack of differentiation results in conflict and/or loss of intimacy, both of which can lead to sexual problems and even break-ups. As therapy progressed for Tim and Amanda, they came to realize that this was actually their core issue. Sure, they needed to learn how to communicate more effectively so they could discuss things they disagreed on. But as they started to confront *what* they disagreed on — things like how often they had sex and the way they did it, how often they went out socializing, how they planned to transition into their 'empty nest' years and so on — they came face to face with their own individual difficulties backing themselves and asking for their needs to be met, especially when the other person held a different agenda or was trying to change them.

Mindfulness helps us develop differentiation. As we explored above, when we learn to identify our needs and boundaries and express these directly to our partner and other people we are close to, we become more able to stay in proximity to others without losing a sense of ourselves. Clients of ours regularly report feeling somehow more 'real' and 'solid' as they learn to do this. They report experiencing a capacity to be truthful and to be themselves and this contributes to a sense of authenticity in the relationship as well as generating more passion.

Differentiation begins with learning to pause. This slows things down and allows us to sense inside to notice what is true for us. This was the first step in therapy for Tim and Amanda. They both needed to learn how to pause and stop reacting with blame and withdrawal. Like pressing pause on a movie, suddenly they became aware that they were caught up in stories and reactions rather than seeing each other clearly. Mindfulness meditation is an example of a pause, but it is important to keep in mind that we don't have to stop for five minutes. Simply taking a single mindful breath, feeling our feet on the ground for a single moment, or otherwise just intentionally taking time to reconnect with the body can often be all it takes. Doing so puts a break in the transmission, we step out of default mode and we have the possibility of responding to the situation on its merits rather than simply reacting according to our previous conditioning. When Tim and Amanda started pausing during times of conflict, they immediately became less reactive.

They also learnt to deepen the pause by sensing into themselves and inquiring into what needs were not getting met and/or what boundaries were being crossed. In the beginning, they had to sit quietly by themselves and do this — both in therapy and in their own time. However, as they practised doing this it became easier (like everything we practise) and soon they found they were at times able to do it in the middle of an argument. Armed with this new skill, they started finding ways to express their needs more directly and to hold onto themselves when the other person was unable or unwilling to meet these.

Pausing helps us access our inner wisdom, which in turn helps us know how to respond. When we start taking responsibility for our own vulnerabilities rather than trying to change the people around us to accommodate them, we are able to express our deepest truth and live in that, regardless of how it is received. This is an important point. We express our vulnerability and request to have our needs met even when we do not get validated in that request or expression of vulnerability. In effect we learn to soothe ourselves and say what we need even if there is a fear of rejection. We find we do not need to pretend by only allowing the 'nice' feelings to be shown. We develop a sense of trust in our capacity to speak the truth and to create healthy boundaries. When we take responsibility for our own feelings we can use 'I' statements rather than blame. And we can be brave and courageous in our relationships because we are not acting out old patterns and reactivity. We become able to respond rather than react, and gain a sense of responsibility, autonomy and wisdom. We can be increasingly present with ourselves and others. And when we relax we can feel a sense of openness rather than rigidity, and feel calmer and more compassionate. The more we practise this, the less we find that our own emotional state fluctuates in response to the moods of others around us.

Empathy and compassion

Holding space rather than reacting lets us stay present and we thus start seeing things more clearly. In time, we become aware of our partner's unique triggers and vulnerabilities and recognize their reactivity as attempts to cope with these things when they feel unsafe. This is the basis of genuine empathy. Our insula starts to stay online even when we feel threatened, meaning we can remain simultaneously aware of what is happening for our partner and ourself. Recognizing this and greeting our partner's vulnerability with loving presence is the most healing thing we can do in relationship. Ultimately we must each learn to give this to ourself, but it helps when partners also give each other the gift of loving presence when the other is feeling vulnerable.

When young children experience overwhelming emotions,

what they need is for a parent or some other adult to validate the emotion, give them permission to have it, and stay present with them. Physical gestures of kindness and touch, soothing reassurance that things will be okay, or even just sustained presence all help children to be with their emotions. This provides a container for the emotion — a sense of something bigger than the emotion. And this is what makes it okay to have the emotion. With repeated experiences of this we start to internalize this relationship. That is, we come to relate to our own emotional reactions in this way — bringing an attitude of loving presence, which keeps our insula and prefrontal cortex engaged. The result is that we 'have our emotions' rather than 'our emotions having us'. We recognize that we are not our emotions but that we are separate from them. When we know this, it feels safer for us to feel our feelings because we are not so completely identified with them. We recognize that feelings come and go but that we are still fundamentally okay, regardless of what passes through us.

However, for many of us there were times when this loving adult figure was not available. Perhaps we were physically alone or maybe our parent was physically present but caught up in their own insecurities or some other difficulty that made it impossible for them to bring loving presence to us. Perhaps they failed to notice our distress or reacted with frustration. Or perhaps they tried to talk us out of having it with a well-meaning 'It's okay … don't worry about it'. In these situations we were left alone with our distress. In the absence of a loving, present container we naturally developed coping strategies such as avoidance, distraction, repression or being tough on ourselves. If this happened often enough, we internalized *these* and this became how we related to our own distress.

Later, when we found ourselves in intimate relationships, how do you think we related to our partner's distress and vulnerability? This is what was happening for both of the couples we have met so far in this book. Obviously, if we haven't developed the resource of being able to hold our own distress in a space of mindfulness and loving presence, we will be unable to do this for anyone else. This is why genuine intimacy begins with us and then radiates out to others. We can learn to re-parent ourselves and can then bring this relationship to our partner.

EXERCISE: LISTENING DEEPLY AND DEVELOPING EMPATHY

Take some time to offer to be with your partner and really listen to what they have to say. Invite them to talk about something that they find difficult.

Pause and listen deeply, without trying to fix anything. Sense the underlying emotions. You might pay attention to their body language and their facial expressions as well as the words they use and the tone of voice.

Reflect back to them what you understand them to be saying. Check that you have understood correctly and when you are really sure that you understand them perhaps summarize what they have said.

Then imagine what it would be like to be in their shoes. Say something simple like, 'You must feel so frustrated about that ...' or 'That must make you feel really sad.' Notice how they react and see if you can read whether you have been accurate. Then ask them whether you were, and compare their response to what you thought.

Remember: the goal is not to solve their problem, rather to let them know that you understand. Building the bridge of empathy is crucial for healthy relationships. It's the part that is so often missing but when it is there we feel safe, like we can come home to each other.

This exercise may feel artificial or contrived at first, if we are not used to communicating this way. However, with practice it becomes easier and more natural.

When we are able to realize that our partner's reactions are just attempts to deal with feeling vulnerable — using whatever resources they internalized as a child — we become less likely to react and add fuel to the fire. When we learn to hold their vulnerability in a space of loving presence, their deepest, most vulnerable parts feel safe and calm down. When conflict arises both partners can speak to what is good in the other rather than identifying with (and feeding) each other's defences. We are not talking here about condoning bad behaviour. Instead, we are pointing to the importance of having compassion for our own suffering when there is conflict and then extending this to our partner. When both partners have the intention to do this wherever possible, the relationship becomes more authentic and loving. At times, one partner might have to hold space while the other relaxes into their vulnerability, and later these roles may reverse. This is the basis of healthy relationships.

EXERCISE: HUGGING MEDITATION

Stand, sit or lie embracing your partner. Breathe in and hold them in their entirety. Breathe out and let them hold you.

After going back and forth doing this for a while, drop this intention and simply hug each other until you both relax.

CHAPTER 8
Mindful sex

Think about the best sex you have ever had. Go on — let yourself really relive the experience! Take a moment to remember what it felt like in your body, what emotions were evoked and what was happening in your mind. Chances are you were really *there* while you were having it — fully in your body. You were most likely mentally and emotionally connected to your partner, in addition to the physical connection. If we recall the Killingsworth and Gilbert smartphone study we mentioned on page 12, even their participants were present nearly all of the time when they were having sex (which is significantly more than the 53.1 per cent, which was average during all other activities)!

Now recall some average or lacklustre sex you have had. Again, take some time to recall the physical, emotional and mental aspects of the experience. What was different? What is the difference between sex and *great sex*?

You may have noticed during that exercise that it is pleasurable just to think about sex, whether it was good or bad. After all, there is that joke that it is like pizza — that even when it's bad it's still good. But you would have noticed an obvious difference between the two experiences. And then, to make the distinction even more obvious, there is the realm of *really* bad sex — ranging from the awkward and disconnected through to 'think about something (or someone) else until it's over' experiences, all the way to those really scarring experiences that so many people sadly carry as part of their sexual history.

So what is it that makes for truly great sex? And what is it that is lacking when sex is average or bad? As we have explored at length throughout *Mindful Relationships*, one of the main things that defines the quality of *any* relationship — whether with ourselves or with those around us — is intimacy. And perhaps nowhere is the importance of intimacy more obvious than when it comes to sex. The ability to be present, open and in our body is fundamental to having a good sex life. Nowhere else are we more exposed and vulnerable. As a result, sex can be either an incredibly healing experience, as we are seen and loved fully for who we are, or a terrifying and even damaging one, when we are seen and somehow rejected — or not seen at all in the first place. And even sexual relationships that start out as uncomplicated can eventually run into problems such as reduced desire. This is particularly prevalent once couples get busy with their careers and especially when they have children. In this chapter we explore ways emotional intimacy leads to greater sexual intimacy, and how mindfulness can aid this process. We will also explore common sexual problems that we see in our therapy practices and ways that mindfulness can help us to reclaim intimacy in order to have the amazing sex that we desire.

Having a healthy sex life

At its best, sex is joyful and free. When we are able to stay in our bodies during sex, rather than closing down and tuning out, we are able to stay connected to the physical experience of lovemaking. We develop what is called interoceptive awareness, which refers to awareness of our physiological and emotional state. Research shows that increased interoceptive awareness improves sexual experiences by literally getting us out of our heads, reducing anxiety, low mood and self-judgement.[1] As we become aware of our own emotional state and express this physically through lovemaking, we become more attuned to the emotional and physical changes in our partner.[2] We start responding to their moans, changes in breathing, subtle physical changes or a momentary glance. Sex becomes a communication from the deepest parts of us and we can literally connect with the deepest parts of our partner. Some people even describe peak experiences of momentarily losing any sense of where they end and their partner begins. They experience a sense of being one organism. The Kama Sutra, as well as Buddhist and Taoist sexual manuals, all point toward this as being the highest form of lovemaking — indeed, the very *point* of sex. In fact, most experiential religious traditions counsel us toward using sex as a vehicle for transformation and connection. And all emphasize presence and embodiment as the fundamental starting point.

Everything we have just said might seem obvious but you have most likely discovered that it is not always easy to actually achieve. It is common during sex to tune out, dissociate a little and even wander off into thoughts. These thoughts might be about our sexual performance, thinking about work or playing out pornographic scenes in our heads. A number of causes can underlie this tendency, including stress, relationship difficulties and watching too much pornography — all of which make it more likely we will get into our head rather than staying in our bodies.

We are especially likely to disconnect when the emotional connection with our partner deepens and we start to feel vulnerable. We tend to unconsciously choose partners who reflect unresolved relational issues from prior relationships (all the way back to birth) and our past interpersonal relationships significantly impact the way we show up in current relationships. The anxiety that can arise from the experience of having all of this truly seen by someone we care about and don't want to lose can activate the fight/flight/freeze response we explored in Chapter 3. This is of course amplified by any verbal or nonverbal cues of threat from our partner. The amygdala in the left hemisphere picks up on anything threatening in what our partner says and the amygdala in the right hemisphere becomes activated by any nonverbal threat cues, such as a critical or absent tone of voice and changed facial expressions. This amygdala hijack in turn triggers the hypothalamus and sets off a cascade of events in the body and mind, effectively preparing us to neutralize the threat or to flee the situation.

This response is very useful and adaptive when we are faced with a life-threatening situation but is not so great when we are trying to make love to our partner. Under its influence the pituitary glands release cortisol, which impairs our ability to think rationally and to connect emotionally with others.[3] This obviously makes it quite hard to maintain an emotional connection with our partner. Blood flow is redirected away from non-essential functions to the large muscles of the arms and legs, readying us to fight or flee, commonly resulting in loss of erection and vaginal engorgement and lubrication — and a desire to end the sexual encounter. At this point, we become cut off from our own loving emotions and intimacy with our partner becomes impossible. If it is severe enough some people can even numb out and dissociate to the point that they freeze up. Others become aggressive, which can make for some spectacular physical sex, but this generally lacks any sense of intimacy. Think about disappointing sexual experiences you have had. Do you remember experiencing any of these things?

Better sex with mindfulness

To counteract this tendency towards anxiety and fight/flight reactivity we must activate the mammalian tend-and-befriend circuits. As we explored in Chapter 3 these circuits allow us to maintain an emotional connection with others, even when under stress.[4] By simply remaining present during sex we minimize the activation of the fight/flight response. And by focusing on connection and nurturing when stakes are high, we release oxytocin, which helps us to calm down, focus and maintain emotional connection rather than withdrawing or reacting. This response is seen more often in women than men, but can be cultivated with practice by either sex.

EXERCISE: ACTIVATING OUR TEND-AND-BEFRIEND CIRCUITS

Take a moment to pause and sense your way into your body. Notice what sensations are around. Notice any thoughts and simply allow them to come and go. Tune in a little deeper and become aware of your emotional state, simply noting any emotions that are around without judgement or thinking about them. If you can, name the emotional state you are experiencing.

Next, give yourself permission to have the emotion. Recognize that all emotions are normal parts of the human experience and serve a purpose. Pleasant emotions like love, joy and so forth show us that we like what we are experiencing and motivate us to seek experiences like this. On the other hand strong, unpleasant emotions like anger and sadness give us very useful information about needs that are not being met and boundaries that might be being violated.

Say to yourself silently, 'This is [name whatever emotion you are experiencing] and is a completely normal human emotion. It is totally okay that I am experiencing this right now.' Cultivate an attitude of loving acceptance to whatever you are experiencing. Bring this same unconditionally friendly attitude toward any physical sensations and thoughts you are experiencing too.

Now bring to mind people you love — people you care for and who care for you. Perhaps your partner or children, a family member, a friend, even a pet. Take a moment to really sense them in front of you. See their faces, one by one. If there are lots of people who come to mind, hold each in mind for a short time before moving on to the next. If there are moments of hurt or disappointment in the relationship with the people you are sensing in front of you (which is usually the case), just focus here on the sense of love and support.

Tune in to the sense of love and care flowing from you to them and them to you. Take a few moments to really enjoy this feeling. Can you notice the feeling of oxytocin being released? This is what it feels like to be run by our tend-and-befriend circuits.

Practising this exercise regularly when you are calm and relaxed will strengthen the tend-and-befriend circuits. This will then make it easier to activate them when you need them, such as during lovemaking when a button gets pushed and you start to feel vulnerable and reactive. Of course, you can always practise this during sex also — perhaps you and your partner can treat it like a lovemaking meditation. Doing this regularly results in us becoming more relaxed during sex. We become increasingly able to remain connected with our own emotions — and therefore our partner's — and this increases the depth of intimacy during sex.

Making love in this way also ensures the insula remains activated. The insula, as we saw in Chapter 3 (see page 27), is the part of the brain most directly involved in functions such as self-awareness, knowing what is happening interpersonally, and controlling our movement. As such, it is an extremely useful part of the brain for intimacy and lovemaking. And once again, thanks to neuroplasticity, keeping it active by maintaining intimacy with ourselves and others results in stronger connections between the neurons there. Research shows that mindfulness meditation also strengthens the insula, so in a very real sense 'meditators make better lovers'.

Making love in intimate, connected ways — activating the insula and other tend-and-befriend circuitry — literally rewires the brain for deeper intimacy. We become less critical of our (or our partner's) performance, more aware of our breath and body sensations, and more responsive to our partner's body. This then becomes a feedback loop as we then become even more connected with ourselves and our partner. Slowing things down with mindfulness amplifies these benefits. In fact, this is one of the main recommendations that we give anyone who comes to see us in our therapy practices for sexual issues. You can think about it as meditating in missionary, instead of lotus, position!

In the next section we will briefly outline two common sexual issues and how mindfulness can be used to heal them.

Resolving more entrenched sexual issues

Almost without exception, people who turn up for therapy to address sexual problems do so due to issues with intimacy. There's nothing like having sex with someone to bring up all of our unresolved emotional stuff. As we explored in the last section, this tends to activate our fight/flight responses, which hijacks our brain and behaviour. This tends to result in decreased desire for sex and diminished arousal while having it.

Colleen, aged 45, came for therapy frustrated that her sex life with husband Rob was almost non-existent. She felt she had lost the passion and energy she once had. She had started contemplating divorce, although really didn't want to do this. She didn't want to be alone and was worried about disrupting the family in this way. She came to couples therapy reluctantly as she felt intimidated by what it might take to reveal herself in that space. Through being able to have a series of conversations with Rob in therapy she was able to see how, after a number of unsuccessful attempts to negotiate change with him, she had given up on herself and her desires. She realized that her previous attempts to ask for change had been done in a critical way, which Rob reacted to defensively. They had become caught in a cycle of blame and withdrawal. Once this happened, sex was out of the question. Instead they both withdrew and shut each other out. Intimacy was completely closed down and at their worst they stopped even speaking to each other.

Through therapy, Colleen learnt to breathe into her experience, sitting with it long enough that she could see what was going on more clearly. She then took an even deeper breath and started sharing this with Rob. She was able to be vulnerable rather than demanding and critical and she learnt to stand up for what she wanted regardless of the response Rob had. Obviously this took all her powers of mindfulness to calm herself and stay present when her amygdala sensed the potential threat and wanted to hijack things. It also required a great deal of self-compassion, which then naturally extended out towards Rob.

By taking the lead in standing up for what she wanted and signalling to Rob that she was responsible for herself, he began to feel less defensive. He became more comfortable listening and being present for her, as he was no longer feeling so blamed and criticized. When they saw clearly how their relational patterns outside the bedroom led to a loss of intimacy, they were able to generate friendship and healing which led to more willingness to be vulnerable and open to each other in the bedroom.

And then there was Simon, a 42-year-old mechanical engineer. He came to therapy after his wife discovered he had been having a number of affairs and ended the marriage. He had started a relationship with one of the people he had been cheating on his wife with, but then began having trouble maintaining an erection. In fact, after some time he had trouble even getting one in the first place. Like a lot of men, he responded to this issue by going off into fantasies in an attempt to get it up, and put a lot of pressure on himself to do so. Unsurprisingly, this made the situation worse as he became more and more anxious about his sexual 'performance' both during sex and even when anticipating it. Therapy helped Simon to take the pressure off himself and to relax. He took a break from dating and worked on developing greater intimacy with himself, which was something he was naturally cut off from before he came for treatment. As he got more in touch with his deeper wants and needs — and better able to soothe himself when he was emotionally activated — he naturally began to seek out deeper intimacy with the women he was with. He started dating again and took things much more slowly, becoming interested in developing emotional as well as physical connections with women. He relaxed and got back in his body, learnt to talk about his anxiety and the effect it had on his erections. He found that as he did so, he calmed down and his erection problems diminished. He also started having much more intimate, connected sex, which in hindsight was what had been missing in his marriage.

While we used the example of a man here, the same problems occur for women. In fact, lack of emotional intimacy in a relationship tends to be even more of a turn-off for women than men. This comes back to biology and stereotypical relationships that men and women have with sex. Men on the whole are more able to have instrumental sex (just 'getting off') while for women the emotional connections tends to be more important.[5]

EXERCISE: SLOWING DOWN AND CONNECTING DURING SEX

Next time you are making love, focus on foreplay. And here we are not referring to giving amazing head, like some kind of porn star! Instead, we are suggesting you take time to sense your way into your body, getting in touch with your physical and emotional state. You might even like to spend some time meditating (perhaps with your partner) beforehand.

Maintain awareness of your breath. Feel your body against your partner's, really savouring the warmth and softness of the contact. Notice the effect this has on your own body, and see if you can sense the activation of your tend-and-befriend circuits and the release of oxytocin.

If you notice any tension or fight/flight reactivity, focus on breathing and relaxing. You might lose touch with your partner for a moment while you do this but simply reconnect again when you start to feel more relaxed. Keep coming back, over and over, as you would with any mindfulness practice.

If you want to take this way of making love to the next level you can even experiment with looking into your partner's eyes during lovemaking. At first this can be confronting and in some cases even lead to dissociation (where you suddenly feel numb or 'out of your body'). If this happens, you can close your eyes or avert your gaze. But keep coming back to this and develop the ability to maintain eye contact while in close proximity. When you master this you will open up the possibility of extremely intimate — and explosive — sex.

Any time during sex you notice that you are reacting, closing down or tuning out, slow down (or even stop) and bring your attention back to your body. Tune in to your physical sensations, let go of any tension and notice your breath. Then, when you are ready, tune back in to your partner once again — feeling their body touching yours, looking at them (as well as into their eyes) as well as smelling, tasting and hearing them. In this way, lovemaking itself becomes a mindfulness practice.

The strategies explored in this chapter have worked for many people and you might find that they very quickly improve your sex life. Simply being more present and relaxed could be all you need. However, if you (or your partner) have sexual or intimacy problems that don't improve even after trying some of these strategies, you might like to explore therapy as an option. Both individual and couple's counselling with a good therapist can be very beneficial.

CHAPTER 9

When things go wrong

So far in *Mindful Learning* we have explored how mindfulness can help us cultivate the intimacy we desire to create strong, healthy relationships. Along the way, we have looked at how to deal with different challenges as they arise, including major developmental tasks such as differentiation. In this chapter we provide some tools for managing difficulties and we look at how mindfulness can help us stay on track and repair breaches in the connection in our relationships.

Taking responsibility and awareness of our own power

As we have seen in previous chapters, when the amygdala takes over and we get caught in fight/flight reactivity, people under stress are inclined to look outwards and to blame the other person or the situation — or even the cat or dog!

Blame is a coping strategy commonly employed when we are unwilling (or unable) to sit with vulnerability. It seems to work because we get to discharge energy, which gives us a sense of release. However, it is corrosive in relationships. A much better strategy is to stay present with what is actually happening. When we sense into what we are feeling about a situation we take back our power. We start to experience things as they actually are, rather than through a fog of reactions and judgements. We become able to sense inwards and our responses become guided by clear seeing, intuition and wisdom. We might not be able to control or choose the outcome of situations but when we are mindful we *can* choose our response. As we sense into our vulnerability, we also become able to directly express our needs rather than speaking or acting reactively. Vulnerability researcher Brené Brown points out that being able to do this means we can hold people accountable for their actions that hurt us. We can then have a conversation with them about it rather than getting bogged down in blame.

With mindful presence and awareness comes a sense of choice, as we recognize that in each moment of awareness there is also opportunity for growth. In her book *Practicing Peace*, Pema Chödron says the following about choice:

> *If you have embarked on this journey of self-reflection, you may be at a place that everyone, sooner or later, experiences on the spiritual path. After a while it seems like almost every moment of your life you're there, where you realize you have a choice. You have a choice whether to open or close, whether to hold on or let go, whether to harden or soften, whether to hold your seat or strike out. That choice is presented to you again and again and again.*

By staying present in difficult situations we become able to sense our wisdom and intuition about what is the best course of action.

This allows us to respond appropriately to what is happening, drawing on our values and integrity.

Repair

Do you need to be right, to always win the argument? If so, have you noticed how much you sacrifice connection and intimacy because of it? By holding rigidly to our position we miss out on our own happiness. If we focus on being right we miss the opportunity for empathy and for connecting to the vulnerability beneath the surface, which is the place where we can really connect. And knowing how to repair ruptures in intimacy with others is crucial. Research shows that the absence of repair leads to increased levels of resentment and ultimately contempt in relationships. And marriage expert John Gottman has found contempt to be a factor in predicting divorce.[1]

The first step in rectifying a loss of connection is recognizing and acknowledging that things have gone wrong. We need to give ourselves permission to go into fight/flight mode. This is a survival response conditioned over tens of thousands of years that is naturally triggered when we sense threat. Giving ourself this permission takes the pressure off and we can then use mindfulness to help re-engage the tend-and-befriend circuits.

When we are aroused and triggered our medial prefrontal cortex — the part of the brain responsible for introspection — goes offline. The amygdala takes over and we start scanning for problems. As we give our attention to this task, this feeds our anxiety and we inevitably start finding problems, either within or outside of ourselves. This leads to self-criticism and blame, respectively. Trauma expert Janine Fischer says simply being mindful enough to recognize and say 'I'm being triggered' can head off a lot of this reactive behaviour and prevent things spiralling in a negative direction.

When we stay present and open and search for ways to resolve the situation we notice our capacity to stay simultaneously aware of both our own reactions as well as what is happening around us. When we acknowledge what we are feeling and make room for it, we are also more able to make room for what the other person is feeling. Then we are able to see if there is something we have done to contribute to the problem. And we can then bring an attitude of friendliness and compassion to the conflict, which serves to calm things down. As the dust settles a bit, we become able to more accurately discern the response that is likely to resolve the conflict. This discernment, which comes from seeing the situation clearly rather than through a fog of default mode reactivity, is very different from ego-based judgements. It is a very useful side effect of being mindful.

All this may sound like a lot of work. However, as we systematically develop our mindfulness we automatically develop the capacity to stay present and clear, even in situations of conflict and stress. We can then gradually become more aware of our beliefs and less unconsciously driven by them. We know that by taking responsibility for our part and because we care for the other person, we can immediately take steps to bring healing as soon as we know there is a need for it. We cannot make the other person respond in ways we would like but we can acknowledge our own part.

As we said previously this does not mean we are passive or accommodate bad behaviour. This is a very important point. Sometimes people hear the word 'acceptance' and think this means resignation or allowing others to cause us harm. On the contrary, mindfulness gives us the power to speak up or at least to discern when to speak or when not to. When things go wrong we are better off being able to realistically assess the situation so that we can see and consider options. We do not have to get lost in the drama of our stories and when we do we simply notice that (without judgement), then bring ourselves back to the present moment again and again. Making amends and choosing not to hold a grudge are all options available to us. We create and generate new options from an attitude of willingness to turn towards each other rather than away and to say sorry for our part in conflict. Repair means that we take responsibility for maintaining the bond in relationship, we can initiate this and respond to it in loving and friendly ways.

Asking for and taking space

One way to think about mindfulness practice is that it gives us space from our fight/flight reactivity. This is a metaphor obviously, but speaks to the way mindfulness helps us move from automatically believing — and acting on — our thoughts and emotions to experiencing them as mental events and patterns of physical sensations. When we do this we stay present and activate our prefrontal cortex and tend-and-befriend circuits. With practice we become able to do this even in high-stake situations and moments of conflict.

However, at times we might be unable to hold onto ourselves. In these moments we may need to take *physical* space so we can calm down again and reconnect with loving presence. This might require five minutes while we go and make a cup of tea, or a few hours while we go for a walk and calm down. Sometimes we even need to sleep on it or take a few days to process it.

However long we need, what is important is that we negotiate taking space beforehand. If we just bail in the middle of an argument, our partner can experience this as abandonment or withdrawal used as punishment. But if we have a prior agreement that we will each take responsibility for our emotions — and take space when we can't use mindfulness to stop ourselves from reacting — our partner is more likely to experience our leaving as a genuine attempt to resolve the conflict in an adult way. Equally important is that we have an agreement that we will *return* once we have calmed down. If we don't return, this becomes a pattern of avoidance where the issue is just ignored or swept under the rug. So many couples fall into this trap, with the result that resentment builds and leaks out in other areas of the relationship or causes major blow-ups. Agreeing with our partner that we will take space to calm down when we sense an imminent amygdala hijack and then return once we have reengaged our prefrontal cortex and tend-and-befriend circuits makes for much more conscious fighting and conflict resolution. This needs to be established as a rule for fair fighting.

Carol and Jack were clients who presented for couple's therapy. They had been married for eleven years and had three children. Both had been deeply unhappy in the marriage for some time. They invariably dealt with conflict by pretending it had not happened and sweeping it under the rug. They felt powerless to do anything about the cycle of rejection, withdrawal, blame and attack they were caught in. They did not want to continue down this unhappy road nor did they want to end the relationship. Both believed the other was at fault. 'Saying sorry,' said Carol, 'when I haven't done anything wrong just means Jack can do it all again and believe me, I know Jack and he will.' Jack in turn responded, 'Yes, that's just how you always are, blaming and critical. I feel as if no matter what I do I will never please you.'

Letting go of believing we are right can bring up a lot of fear for people in situations like this but refusing to do so keeps us stuck in a cycle of conflict, just like Carol and Jack. When we bring mindfulness to the pattern and inquire into what is going on, we can start to see how we have held onto ways of being that contribute to hurting others in our relationships. An opening and softening can occur. It came as a surprise to Carol and Jack that underneath their stories they were both feeling unlovable and fearful of being left alone. They missed the good things that each offered because they were caught in their habitual story of unworthiness and a deep-down sense of not being good enough. In effect, their brains had become conditioned to expect the worst and they were constantly on high alert around each other. In the rare moments they managed to be friendly and loving to each other, neither was able to trust this or to take it in. For instance, when Carol requested Jack cuddle her, he refused if he did not *feel* their closeness was genuine. He was stuck in a self-perpetuating cycle and then missed the opportunity to rebuild that closeness, which of course then made Carol feel even more vulnerable and rejected. Nor did Jack make bids of his own to reconnect. Neither was able to soothe each other's hijacked amygdalae or their own and they stayed stuck in patterns of rejection, anger and withdrawal. They missed each other's bids for increased intimacy and for repair.

Mindfulness allows us to be with whatever is happening with a sense of friendly compassion. We simply breathe into patterns of fear and blame. A simple acknowledgement of our part in the dance can create a ripple effect that brings change in unexpected ways. By bringing an attitude of friendliness and compassion we start to calm down and see things more clearly. We may see why we or our partner might have acted in hurtful ways. This defuses the hostility and our brains and bodies can settle, allowing for even clearer seeing. The sense of threat subsides and it becomes easier to simply offer an apology or other gestures of kindness and connection.

As they progressed in therapy and began communicating more effectively, Carol and Jack learnt that they needed to take care of this third entity called 'The Relationship'. They came to see that working out who was at fault was much less important than developing a sense of awareness of their own contributions to the dance they found themselves in. Carol saw that her pattern was to feel unheard and then become critical in a misguided attempt to get Jack to take her more seriously. This was a pattern she had learnt in childhood from parents whose only interactions with her tended to involve direct or implicit criticism of her behaviour. She then internalized this attitude and related to her own vulnerabilities with self-criticism. And the more she criticized Jack, the more he felt attacked and withdrew. Carol's critical stance was preventing Jack from being present and available in the ways she wanted, and his tendency to withdraw exacerbated the issue. They had in effect adopted a pursuer–distancer pattern, which is common in intimate relationships.

As they became clearer about their communication patterns, both became aware that apologizing somehow felt akin to a loss. In order to resolve things, this reaction needed to be traced to its origins. This is how good therapy tends to work — as we deal with what is presenting itself on the surface, deeper issues start to arise. Most of us carry wounds from our childhood that show up in our relationships and keep us stuck. Learning to recognize these wounds and how they influence our behaviour can help us work more skilfully with them. It can also be affirming and healing to see that dysfunctional patterns we have are just ways we developed to survive difficulties earlier in life, when we didn't have the resources to deal with it any other way. This makes it easier to let go of these defences in the present and to develop more mature, adaptive ways of getting our needs met.

While we tend to enter into relationships at the same general level of differentiation as our partner, at any one time one person is usually more able to grow and change the relationship than the other. This tends to go back and forth over time. That is the dance of relationships. However, in some relationships one partner might be more inclined overall to seek deeper intimacy or resolve issues. 'Why should I be the one?' is a common enough response to which the answer may well be 'Why not?' Sometimes it takes a unilateral effort or stand by one partner to force change in the system. The other partner can then engage in the change process, or resist it. It then becomes necessary for the partner desiring change to continue to hold onto themselves and push for what they need.

However, in the case of Carol and Jack they both recognized that the first step was for each to take responsibility for their own part in the dance. They didn't always manage to do this, nor was progress linear. Like all change it was often two steps back and one forward. They did feel impatient at times and they did keep hurting each other — *at first*. However, by recognizing that they could rectify matters and take steps to mend a lack of connection as soon as they noticed it, they developed much more harmony in their relationship. They became quicker at recognizing when things were going pear-shaped and more effective at doing something about it.

By committing to change just ourselves and by being open to contact our deepest awareness of ourselves, we can allow ourselves to be vulnerable and human. When Carol shared with Jack her fear of not being heard and her sense that she wasn't important to him,

Jack in turn was able to share his own vulnerability — his sense of failure and the many ways in which he was blaming himself for disappointments in their lives and how things had turned out. He was able to see that he was shutting down because he felt criticized and judged by Carol, and because of his own self-judgements. He was able to speak from this vulnerable place rather that getting defensive and attacking. He became able to experience her requests for physical affection as a desire to connect with him rather than a judgement about his unavailability and started responding more generously. By sharing their vulnerability they were able to see each other through a compassionate lens. They developed the capacity to listen to each other and to be empathic.

Although a sincere apology can go a long way in bringing healing in a relationship, saying sorry is not the only way to repair ruptures. There are many ways to communicate love, affection and friendship both to ourselves and our partner. By turning inwards and finding the capacity within to offer kindness in whatever form is needed, we shift the focus. By simply holding an intention to be kind, and then taking whatever action we need to, we become bigger than the behaviours that might otherwise define us. And as we become aware of our pain, whether because of the judgements of others or of our own harshness with ourselves, we can offer a gesture of compassion. We might put a hand on our heart to soothe ourselves or we might offer a hand or gesture of touch to our partner when they are in distress.

By taking responsibility for our own part in the dance, the dance itself changes. We stop stepping on our partner's toes and tripping over our own feet. We realize that by focusing on how we aspire to be in the relationship, rather than what our partner is doing (or not doing), we paradoxically often affect the change we desire.

We become agents of change in the relationship rather than passive victims. We become empowered by a capacity to stay grounded, present and loving, and reclaim our own power.

Fighting fair

John Gottman has shown that conflict is inevitable in relationships, and it is how we manage it that determines the health of the relationship. Practising mindfulness is a crucial first step as it helps us prevent fights from escalating and to see clearly. Where there are continual cycles of negativity and fights that go nowhere we need to develop rules and agreements around fighting and set out what is acceptable. And it can be helpful to look deeply at what the fighting is really about as usually it is representative of a deeper concern than what seems to be the issue at hand.

The first step in fighting effectively is learning to pause. Whenever we detect reactivity in ourselves or our partner, we should stop what we are saying or doing and reconnect with our senses. As we repeatedly pause in the middle of patterns of reactivity, we can start making better choices. We can also ask ourselves, 'How can I use mindfulness to pay attention to my partner in a way that might resolve the conflict?' Doing this helps us drop any agenda other than staying present, seeing what is true, and resolving things in a way that both people are happy with. We can then connect with the loving presence in our partner and focus on resolving the conflict rather than winning the argument. Gottman's research also shows that *accepting* that some conflict in relationships is unsolvable fosters better relationships. When we know that not everything can be worked out, mindfulness helps us accept this and still stay connected to our partner.

When we drop assumptions and have an open mind set about what's possible, our relationships unfold and evolve in new and fresh ways. A good intention to have is that the relationship is a no-negativity zone and that each person has permission to remind the other when this is forgotten! This sets up a foundation and then further to this we can create rules such as no name-calling or attacking with nasty or vitriolic comments, no yelling etc. The idea here is to develop boundaries around what is acceptable and tolerable for you. Finally, looking at each other while fighting helps keep the prefrontal cortex engaged and reduces amygdala hijack. This is why it is far better to have arguments face to face than via the phone, text or email.

To return to Carol and Jack, they made an agreement to come back to each other within a short time if there had been a fight so as their pattern of sweeping conflict under the carpet was no longer an issue. This created a sense of safety and protected their bond. They resolved to each take the time to listen to how the other was feeling without interrupting. They started to look at each other with compassion as they began to share more of their vulnerability. Simply by committing to this one step of coming back to each other to resolve or at least dialogue about conflict, they stopped fearing that either one would leave. This sense that they would each listen to and respect each other had a ripple effect. It didn't mean that conflict disappeared from their relationship, but both felt more secure with each other. As they in turn began to care for each other better they also started caring for the relationship itself.

You might experiment with your own rules and see what you need to feel safe so that you can repair the ruptures more quickly when they happen. If you are looking at yourself and your partner through the eyes of mindfulness you will be kinder and more compassionate. Making a commitment to reduce negativity and be prepared to see each other's perspective could be a good start.

EXERCISE: LEARNING HOW TO FIGHT FAIR

First, recognize that disagreements and fights are inevitable in any relationship. The trick is to learn to do it effectively.

Pick a calm time when you are not fighting to discuss what the fights might mean and look underneath to see what they represent.

For example, do you fight about money? Maybe you are worried about your future security or about losing a sense of control. Do you each have different attitudes to spending and saving and if so where do these come from?

Do you fight about children? If so, discuss how were you raised and what your values are around childrearing.

If you fight about how each person spends their time, what are your expectations and hopes for connection and intimacy?

Spend time listening deeply to each person's point of view and make some rules about the discussions. You might like to decide ahead of time that neither will interrupt the other. You might agree not to be negative, blaming or critical but to listen with a sense of curiosity as you really try to understand where each other is coming from.

Experiment with establishing your own ground rules for fairness, particularly around loaded issues.

CHAPTER 10
Seeking help

By now you should have a good idea of how to use mindfulness to create strong, healthy relationships — and to identify and resolve problems as they arise. However sometimes issues arise in relationships that we are unable to resolve ourselves, or through discussion with friends and family.

Knowing when and how to seek help

According to relationship expert John Gottman most couples wait too long before seeking help in their relationship. This can be as long as six or seven years, which is a long time for people in relationship distress. These days it is less of a taboo than it used to be to talk about relationship difficulties, but still for some, seeing a therapist feels like an admission of failure.

There is no shame in seeking help. In fact, knowing when a third party is required to help resolve an impasse is a strength. It takes wisdom and courage to seek help from a professional such as a counsellor or therapist, and couples generally experience a great sense of relief when they can discuss their problems with a neutral third person and find tools and support to change their relationship patterns. Especially if they have been in pain for a long time it is encouraging to learn that there are things they can do. We have highlighted a number of cases of people throughout the book so far who achieved great benefits from seeking therapy, either individually or as couples.

In any situation it is important to know when to ask for help and relationships are no different. We get support through life in a whole range of fields such as financial, health, medical, nutritional advice, and acknowledging our need for relationship support is not an acknowledgement of failure but rather a mark of maturity. Good couple's therapy provides a space where we can safely explore what is really happening in the relationship. We can also learn new skills that we may not have discovered ourselves through trial and error. It can empower us to become agents of change in our own lives. This chapter is about knowing when to seek help, finding a good therapist and encouraging our partner to engage in therapy.

Getting some good couple's therapy can often mean the difference between separating and turning your relationship around in a completely different direction. Or if one person is unsure about having couple's therapy and thinks they might want to end the relationship, it is good to see a therapist who specializes in discernment counselling, which is different again from couple's therapy. This is a valuable process which allows couples to look at what has gone wrong so that they can manage their future relationship better, especially where children are involved, and also gather the information they need to decide whether to work on the relationship. It is especially useful where one person might want to work on the relationship and the other person is not sure about whether to end it. And even if after discernment counselling, couples still decide to separate, they will at least be able to do so with more awareness so that they do not take the same patterns into their next relationships. There is a saying, 'Wherever you go, there you are', and we find that couples learn significant things about themselves and their partners in therapy which often come as a surprise and which equip them not only in their intimate relationships but also more generally in life. In the event that it becomes necessary to separate, collaborative family law offers couples a unique process in which to separate mindfully. This is a process that offers couples the opportunity to decide for themselves what is important rather than have a court decide as well as have the support of a skilful team of practitioners that support all aspects of separation, especially the emotional component. Couples are supported in transitioning into new families with an emphasis on what each person needs and with a focus on children and relationships.

Getting our partner on board

By now you will hopefully understand how futile blame is in relationships. Using blame to coerce your partner into a therapist's office is not likely to work. Instead, recognizing that the dance you are in is created by both of you engenders kindness and compassion. This makes it easier to recognize that your partner is suffering too, and to frame the need for counselling as a wise move to get support rather than a way to fix or change them. It could be that it is for your own benefit or for both of you. After all, one person might not believe there is a problem. So, it is wise to be able to communicate without complaining or blaming.

You might like to start by giving your partner a heads up that there is something you want to talk about — that way they won't feel ambushed. Then when you have agreed on a good time to talk, start by telling them what you *like* about the relationship. Then explain what you find challenging and would like to resolve in therapy. Do this in a way that takes responsibility for your own actions and experiences, rather than blaming them. Even if you think that it is all your partner's fault, it isn't. Relationships are co-created and we all play a part in what works and what doesn't.

Be prepared to listen to your partner's perspective, maybe about why they don't want to see a therapist and try to really understand their position. When you have really listened you can try to see if you have understood by saying something like, 'Let me see if I have understood you properly — you don't want to go and just get blamed for all the problems' or 'You don't want to go and pay good money to just keep having the same old fights' or 'You are a very private person and you don't want to air our dirty linen in public'. Invite your partner to offer corrections and clarifications so you can be sure you understand them — and so they know you understand. Then you might respond by reassuring them that you are not wanting to blame or to continue fighting, that you understand that money is tight, or whatever the issue is. Really seek to walk in their shoes *and* reiterate the reasons that you think therapy is a good idea. Speak to what could be possible in the relationship.

We suggest you say that you feel as if you need some tools and techniques to help with the 'stuckness' or the patterns and ask if they would be willing to come to at least one session to see how it goes. You might suggest that together you do some research to find a therapist who will suit both your needs. Take it slowly and be prepared to listen, to validate, to see your partner's point of view but also to hold steady on your own and not capitulate or accommodate. Explain that you cannot see another way for the two of you to get a better relationship. You might say, 'It makes sense that you don't want to go for the reasons you expressed … I really admire that you are independent and want to fix it ourselves but we're not doing too well with that on our own and I'm concerned. Our marriage needs help and let's at least give it a try and see after one session what we both think.' You might think about this as creating a clearing and invite your partner to step into that. In the dense forest of conflict and misunderstanding, one partner can make a unilateral stand for resolution and invite their partner to join them. You can't force them, but you can shine plenty of sunlight on the clearing you have created and make it as appealing as possible. At the same time, you can take a very firm stand. But again, stand for a more intimate, loving relationship, rather than standing for your partner to agree to your demands.

A differentiated stance

Having said all of this, at times our partner may be unwilling to budge. In these moments, we are faced with a difficult choice. Do we give in and allow things to continue as they are, or do we keep pushing for change? A differentiated stance here is to unilaterally push for change. This might take the form of refusing to let the issue drop or having some therapy yourself, or even making the decision to leave if they do not agree to therapy. If you take the latter path, don't do it as a way of manipulating your partner into therapy — they will pick up on this and you will find yourself in a power struggle. Mindfully holding onto ourselves while maintaining a stance of loving friendliness even in the face of resistance and sitting in that space is what works. And, it becomes up to *us* to unilaterally decide what we are going to do. We can keep offering to go to therapy every step of the way, even after we have separated. This is in fact what ended up happening for Tim and Amanda. After some good early progress in therapy, Tim became afraid of what it would mean to assume a genuinely differentiated stance, and started returning to patterns of blame and withdrawal. Even though he could see what was happening, he refused to budge. Amanda was then forced to make a tough choice — allow him to dictate the terms of their relationship, or leave. After much soul-searching (including some time at a silent meditation retreat), she made the difficult decision to leave the marriage. Since she recognized that she would always be in a relationship with Tim (as the father of their children), she asked him to continue therapy so they could separate mindfully. Tim ultimately refused, in line with his general pattern of avoidance, but Amanda attended a few more sessions by herself at various points over the next year as she found ways of separating in a way that was conscious and healthy.

Imagine what sort of relationship you want to create

People we see in our therapy practices often have vague ideas of what the problems are. Very often everything is thrown under the almighty label of 'communication problems'. They have general ideas but these need to be broken down into specific behaviours. We cannot get to where we want to get to without a roadmap. We are creating our own relationship anyway, so we may as well create something that we actually want to create. Knowing you want change is one thing; having a vision for your relationship is another!

EXERCISE: KNOWING WHAT YOU WANT IN RELATIONSHIP (AND USING THIS TO INVITE YOUR PARTNER INTO THERAPY)

Take some time to become present. (You might like to refer back to earlier exercises on how to become present.) Pause and sense inwards as you become aware of your breathing.

Once you have sensed your way into your body and your mind has quietened a little, drop an inquiry into that space. Ask yourself 'What is my deepest aspiration for this relationship? What does my heart desire most?' Sit with this inquiry. Don't try to work out an answer as this will keep you on a conscious level, where you are likely to recreate what you have always thought and done. Instead, allow a sense of what is *truly* important to you to arise from somewhere deep inside.

Take your time and really give the question space. If your mind wanders, just keep coming back to the inquiry, 'What is my deepest aspiration for this relationship? What does my heart desire most?'

Whatever comes up, hold this in mind as a vision for the potential for your relationship. Then share this with your partner. You might even like to do this exercise together.

Finding a therapist

Ideally, you might look together for a therapist and brainstorm about how to do this. Have you heard of someone good through friends, or do you want to search online? Usually most therapists will offer you a brief chat when you make the initial call so that you can get an idea of how they work. You may even do this together and put the phone on speaker so you can both ask whatever questions you have.

Be prepared to spend some time looking to see if you can find a therapist who feels like the right fit for you. And feel free to change therapists after a session or two if you don't feel they are a good match for you both. We hear complaints about therapists in our offices which include therapists taking sides, being too passive and listening endlessly without offering suggestions or tools, being too focused on techniques and failing to stop the fighting. It is an individual thing and no one size fits all, so it is worth finding a person with whom you both feel comfortable. There are many different styles and approaches to couple's therapy and your relationship with your therapist should feel like a good match. However, if you don't find the right therapist at first, don't give up. If you took your car to one mechanic who didn't do a good enough job you would search for a better one. You wouldn't decide that taking the car to a mechanic is a waste of time. If you are reading this book you will know that your relationship matters and it's worth persevering to find good support.

PART 4

The mindful family

CHAPTER 11

Mindful parenting

As parents, we can feel pushed and pulled in many directions at the same time. No one prepared us for how hard it can be. As life gets busier and more stressful generally, the demands of raising a family can at times feel overwhelming. How do we stay calm in the face of all the conflicting pressures of family life? The new baby who never seems to sleep. The child who bites, kicks or screams at us. The fighting and bickering that always seems to happen while we are trying to manage the household or make work calls. On top of this we might have financial stress or health issues. And our children themselves are facing unprecedented academic, social and societal pressures that many of us never had to face when we were young, meaning that we can often be at a loss to guide them in navigating these challenges.

As we have explored throughout this book, practising mindfulness facilitates self-awareness and self-compassion and enhances our capacity to be present. These skills enhance our parenting. To return to our ripple metaphor, if we are able to hold our own inner experience in a space of loving presence, this is naturally extended outwards into our family. When we as parents are mindful, our kids tend to become mindful too, and the whole family becomes infused with presence and friendliness.

But knowing how to balance validating and affirming our children with setting expectations and limits can be very challenging. On the one hand, we want to allow them to develop as individuals and to feel free to explore and express who they truly are. On the other hand, certain limits and boundaries are necessary for them to feel safe and develop appropriately. Especially when children are misbehaving or pushing our buttons it is very important to maintain a sense of loving presence. During these times it is good to remember that kids who feel safe and happy generally don't act out. In fact, if we think about our own behaviour, it is the times when we feel vulnerable and aren't able to hold that vulnerability — or trust that someone else can hold it — that we get defensive. For most of us, feeling vulnerable tends to trigger feelings of fear or shame. If we stay present with these primary emotions, we maintain a sense of integrity and may even be able to express them in a way that ensures our needs are met. However, most of us find this difficult and instead tend to default to secondary emotions as a defence, such as anger, blame or anxiety (which is borne from trying to 'figure everything out'). We are then cut off from our primary emotion and from what we need. If we then judge and react to our secondary emotions, we become even more fragmented.

As we explored in Chapter 6, mindfulness offers a powerful way of re-parenting ourselves. If we bring loving presence to our vulnerability, rather than getting caught up in the layers of reactivity, we literally develop the capacity to make ourselves whole. By learning to, in effect, hold our vulnerable inner child, we heal ourselves. All parts of our personality are given a place, and they all learn to relate to each other with respect and care. We feel whole and integrated, and the internal conflict settles down.

A child's vulnerability

We can bring this same attitude to our children. When they are being naughty or are upset, this tells us that some vulnerability has been triggered in them. What they *don't* need in these moments is condemnation or attempts to 'fix' or distract them from the vulnerability that they are in touch with. When their vulnerability is met with harshness, they have little choice but to go to a defensive strategy such as avoidance or distraction. Or they might attempt to compensate for the vulnerability with perfectionism or dishonesty. Or perhaps they might go to some secondary emotion such as anger, which gives them the illusion of control. Children do this just as adults do.

Even well-meaning attempts to distract or reassure children when they are distressed can cause harm. Think of how common it is for the response 'There, there, it's okay, don't cry' to be used when a child is injured or has their feelings hurt. This attempt at reassurance contains an implicit message that they shouldn't be experiencing what they are experiencing. That is, they are hurting and we are telling them that they aren't (or shouldn't be). On a deep level, this can be very confusing for a child.

Crying is an intense problem-solving strategy that has its roots in our neurobiology. In the first stage of crying our system is on high alert and we are aroused. This stage is known as 'pre-tears'. Take, for example, a child crying in a supermarket who has seemingly lost their mother or father. Initially in this stage, the child is in fight/

flight mode — the sympathetic nervous system is aroused and they are anxious for their safety. Then the parent appears and although there is rapid relief it is accompanied by tears that are an outward manifestation of a shift in body chemistry, which recalibrates the nervous system. This is known as stage two. However, sometimes the parent might say something like, 'Stop crying or I'll really give you something to cry about', which is confusing to the natural problem-solving mechanism of the body.

Instead, what children (and adults) need in these moments is for us to stay present and open with them. We might offer them a hug or some other reassuring touch. Or we might talk in a soothing voice and acknowledge their distress. Children need to be able to feel what they feel without this leading to their parents becoming flooded or overwhelmed. In this way children develop the capacity to become autonomous and to stay connected to themselves. Rather than trying to reason with them or talk them out of what they are feeling, what they actually need is complete acknowledgement of what they are experiencing. It can be useful to encourage the child to name the emotion they are feeling, as this can help them make sense of it and make it feel less scary. If they have trouble naming the emotion, you might name it for them and ask them if the name feels accurate — saying something like, 'You look really angry right now. Are you feeling angry?' You can model with your voice an attitude of curiosity and a sense that it is totally okay for them to be experiencing the emotion they are experiencing. Remember, experiencing an emotion (such as anger) and acting it out (as aggression) are two very different things. Children should be taught this and encouraged to name (but not act out) their emotions.

Bringing this loving presence means that as well as the emotion or vulnerability they are experiencing, the child also experiences something bigger — a safe container of loving presence. You might remember the metaphor of a drop of ink in an ocean, which we discussed in Chapter 6. Over time, with repeated experiences of us being there for them in this way, children internalize this sense of loving presence and learn to relate to their own vulnerable parts in this way. They become able to stay present and friendly with themselves when they are feeling vulnerable, which increases the level of intimacy they have with their own inner world. They become able to sit with their emotions long enough to get familiar with them, improving their emotional literacy and helping them observe the impermanent nature of their emotions — that is, as we have explored throughout *Mindful Relationships*, that emotions come and go when we stop feeding or fighting them. When they are small children, this may look like kneeling on the floor next to them, touching them and offering both acknowledgement of what they are feeling and reassurance that they will be okay. Later on, when they are teenagers, it may look more like asking them if they want to talk about what is troubling them — and reassuring them we are there for them if they want to talk.

It is important to remember here that loving presence is not about allowing bad behaviour. Sometimes the most loving thing a parent can do is to set clear limits and impose consequences. Having clear boundaries actually helps children feel safe, and gives them something to bump up against as they explore who they are in relation to others. And sometimes love takes the form of wrathful compassion — for instance, smacking away a child's hand when they are about to put a knife in the toaster. Sometimes kids need limits set because they do not know what is safe for themselves and others. But together with this we can help them recognize when their behaviour stems from feeling vulnerable, and can help them relate to this vulnerability with love. This is very different from harshly judging their behaviour, which leaves them feeling somehow separate from us and the family, and not okay. Because most of us were not taught this growing up, it can be challenging to parent this way. But as we learn to re-parent ourselves with mindfulness, we can start allowing this same attitude of loving presence to ripple outward to our kids.

Attachment

Infants are completely dependent on their mother or father (or some other primary caregiver) to survive. As a result, they are biologically predisposed to form a close relationship with one or both parents. All attachment styles are about maximizing the amount of care the child receives from this primary caregiver. If care is freely available, children soon learn that they can trust this connection. They become able to tolerate closeness with their parent, such as eye contact and touch, and also separation. If their mother leaves the room, for instance, they will regularly look up from their play to check if she has returned but will remain relatively settled. They trust that she will come back. This is referred to as *secure* attachment.

However, at times the primary caregiver is not fully available to the child. Perhaps they are anxious or reactive. In these cases, the child picks up on the parent's distress and alters their own behaviour so as not to exacerbate this. The child might focus instead on play rather than seeking contact with the parent. This is called *avoidant* attachment. Or perhaps the child will alternate between trying to connect and then disconnecting. This is called *anxious/ambivalent* attachment. In cases where the parent is extremely unwell or unavailable, or in cases of trauma, the child can develop what is called *disorganized* attachment, where they simultaneously approach and retreat from the caregiver and experience a great level of distress.

Whatever attachment style is experienced becomes internalized by the child and forms the basis for how children go on to relate to others throughout their life. Securely attached kids will generally feel safe in later intimate relationships and be able to tolerate closeness and distance without distress. However, insecurely attached children will find themselves feeling anxious, ambivalent or avoidant in later relationships.

Luckily, mindfulness offers a way of re-parenting ourselves. Even though attachment gets encoded early in life, when we learn to bring an attitude of loving presence to our own vulnerability, we are able to undo some of the damage from the early experiences of not getting our needs met or being treated harshly.

Unified parenting

As parents, being on the same page is important. Children have the capacity to cope with their parents having different ways of doing things, but overall parents need to give a consistent message and present a unified front with their kids. Children quickly realize when their parents are not, and learn to exploit this, often playing their parents off against each other in order to get their own way. A certain amount of this happens normally and children are naturally egocentric, but when it is very prominent and becomes the normal way of family relationships there is likely to be resentment and a fall-out from this. When alliances are formed between one parent and children that exclude the other parent, this sets the children up for problems later in life, such as difficulty forming stable couple relationships. The child is likely to feel internal conflict and guilt, feeling disloyal to the other parent. The child is often being used unconsciously to stabilize a parent's feeling of uncertainty and anxiety and this guilt and conflict is internalized in the child.

We cannot overemphasize how important it is for parents to work together as a couple. Obviously there will be times when a child feels closer to one parent or the other, but overall parents need to be a team and support one another rather than collude with a child. Parents should take time to discuss issues together, out of earshot of their children. Then, when they have agreed or reached a compromise on the specific issue, they should return and present a consistent message to their children. It is much harder for kids to oppose a unified front than it is for them to exploit divisions. If you have major differences in values or clashes around parenting that you cannot resolve together, it is a good idea to get some assistance in the form of couple's counselling. It is common for couples to disagree on matters relating to their children and it can be very helpful to unpick this and to see what lies underneath. Often, this is some vulnerability that one or both parents has had triggered by the parenting issue. For instance, your child may be the same age you were when something significant happened in your own life. Or the issue could relate to how you were parented or to a sense that some fundamental values are being disrespected.

Fostering individuality and respect for separateness

Mindfulness practice increases our self-awareness. It also includes the capacity to see our children as separate individuals who are not put on this earth to fulfil our expectations of them but, rather, as precious beings who have their own unique personality and life journey. A common trap for parents is to have unconscious expectations that they project onto their children. These often have nothing to do with the respect for the child as a separate person in his/her own right but are more to do with the disappointments and unfinished business of the parents. It is good here to reflect on your own unexamined beliefs. What hopes and aspirations do we have for our children? Are our aspirations tied up with our own history or are we encouraging them to live their own lives?

Establishing and maintaining boundaries

Respect for separateness means that we are not so identified with our children that we merge with them. Parents need to be at peace within themselves and therefore able to contain but see as separate the feelings of their children. Healthy boundaries are not only about rules, but about knowing who is in charge and who needs to care for whom. Love flows down through the generations, and it is the natural order of things for parents to give to their children. When this flow is reversed, things are out of their natural order. In psychological terms, the child becomes 'parentified' and experiences their emotions as being merged with those of their parents. They do not learn to feel autonomous but rather feel overwhelmed by the demands or emotions of others. An adult who has had this experience will find it difficult to sense into their own emotions. Instead, their default will be to focus on the perceived or imagined (projected) feelings of others. When this becomes a pervasive way of being it becomes difficult to take responsibility for our own feelings and to assert our own needs. This is because our starting point is the responses and reactions of others and this sets up a pattern of pleasing others and potentially we become conflict-avoidant. These children have not had the experience of feeling safely contained by their parents. Mindful parenting allows adults to learn to take responsibility for their own feelings, rather than teach their children to feel guilty if their parents are upset. Mindful parents can say 'I feel sad' rather than 'You made me feel sad'. As we have already mentioned, blame is counter-productive to healthy relationships and so too with our children. When we are able to establish healthy boundaries and to see our children as separate we are more likely to parent from a position of respect and less likely to resort to habitual defensive patterns.

Tom was a father who tended to become impatient and frustrated when three-year-old Mike dawdled around bedtime, which he did often. When Tom reflected on his own experience, he realized that his father had yelled at him and his brothers and that they had had to 'Get to bed … or else.' Bedtime had taken on a threatening tone. When Tom was able to understand what Mike was feeling, he calmed down — and so too did his son. Tom came to see that Mike was in need of some nurturing and reassurance, and saw that his own anger and frustration were not helping the situation. Remember, mindfulness gives us the capacity to sense into ourselves as well as extend the empathy out to another. By reducing the stress in himself, Tom found that Mike calmed down significantly. Tom was able to respond in a more mindful way and also to feel himself to be the parent he wanted to be.

Realistic expectations

It helps to embrace the concept of the 'good enough' parent. We do not need to get it right all of the time. Making mistakes is part of parenting — although it helps if we learn from them!

Having realistic expectations of both ourselves and our children is important. Taking the pressure off ourselves allows us to relax, which makes for better parenting (not to mention a more enjoyable parenting experience). And it is particularly important for our child's development, too. When children expect to be criticized and reprimanded they develop patterns of dishonesty. This becomes a strategy with which they learn to navigate life and to keep others at bay. They grow into adults who feel as if they have to hide parts of themselves. Instead, as parents we need to make it okay for our kids to make mistakes and be honest about them. This way, they can learn from their experience and feel comfortable expressing what is true for them. Mindfulness helps us practise a non-judgemental attitude, which helps us see things more clearly ourselves. When we bring this same attitude to our children, they are able to make sense of their experience without feeling bad about it or as if they need to distort or hide anything.

Brain development

Understanding children's brain development also allows us to have more realistic expectations of them. While there are a number of theories of child development, one of the most widely respected models was developed by Swiss developmental psychologist Jean Piaget.

Piaget noted that children and adolescents go through four key developmental stages. The first of these, which he called the *sensorimotor stage*, occurs from birth to around age two years. During this stage children experience the world almost exclusively through movement and their senses. However, while this may sound like mindfulness at its best, children during this phase are extremely egocentric and unable to experience the world from anyone else's perspective. During this phase, they learn almost exclusively through trial and error. As they approach age two, children develop *object permanence*, meaning they can mentally represent objects. That is, they understand that even though they can't see something (e.g. a toy hidden behind the couch) the thing still exists. At birth, the brain has almost all of the neurons it will ever have, and by age two it is about 80 per cent as large as an adult brain. What mainly changes over the course of development are the connections between the neurons, which become stronger and more complex as learning takes place.

Towards the end of the second year of life, most children enter what Piaget called the *preoperational stage*. It is around this time that children want to know everything and start asking 'Why?' much to the chagrin of their parents! During this stage, from two to seven years, the left hemisphere of the brain undergoes a growth spurt. This hemisphere is responsible for language and other logical, analytical functions. The growth of the left hemisphere therefore allows children to develop language. Their conceptual understanding of the world also goes from being completely illogical to somewhat stable. However, they are still unable to understand concrete logic — facts that are beyond dispute, such as that one plus one equals two. They also remain unable to empathize. This is why it is futile to expect children to share at this stage of their development. They are simply not developmentally capable of putting themselves in another's shoes.

Between the ages of seven and eleven years, during the *concrete operational* stage, children become able to think logically and manipulate ideas in their mind. However, they are still only able to do this with things they can manipulate physically. They also become less egocentric and more logical. This reflects growth spurts that take place in the prefrontal cortex, the control panel of the brain that we have referenced throughout the book.

Finally, from age eleven onwards, they enter the *formal operational* stage. This allows them to develop abstract reasoning and metacognition, or the ability to think about their thinking. Between the ages of fifteen and 25 their prefrontal cortex undergoes a massive growth spurt, allowing adolescents and young adults to think at higher and higher levels of abstraction and to understand their increasingly complex social world. Unfortunately, the parts of the prefrontal cortex that let them regulate their emotional reactions lag a little behind the rest of the prefrontal development, making teenagers more susceptible to emotion regulation problems such as depression and anxiety. This is one of the reasons mental health issues tend to emerge first during this period.

Resilience

Life is not about perfection, and raising children is not all about success. In raising conscious kids, you may like to reflect on which values you wish to pass on and what kind of children you wish to raise. Our children need us to be authentic and to acknowledge where we fail. When we do this we give them a model for authenticity as well as for learning that it is okay to make mistakes. Kids need to fail and, to learn that failure is not to be feared. They need to recover from the inevitable setbacks of life and they need not to be overly protected. Resilient kids are comfortable with who they are and they are not burdened by their parents' expectations of success. Failure teaches them about managing disappointment and teaches them not to expect perfection in others. When parents can openly acknowledge their own failures and humanness, children learn to do this with themselves. They then learn that making mistakes is a necessary part of living a full life. When children see their parents pause and gather themselves during difficult situations, they start doing the same. They learn to respond rather than react and ultimately become empathic citizens, aware of and compassionate towards others. Parents who practise mindfulness are offering a model of persistence. They are teaching that life is about process as well as results.

Handling loss, death and grief

As discussed above, parents need to be able to be real about their own feelings. This includes feelings of loss and grief. Where developmentally appropriate, children need to learn what is true and real. Otherwise they learn to have feelers out like tentacles, always sensing if it is safe and sensing the emotional climate of others around them. Children know intuitively when there is something going on, and denial or attempts to hide important events from them can, at times, leave them confused and unsure whether they can trust their intuition. This can set up a cycle of self-doubt.

Samuel and Olivia were parents in the middle of a divorce. They had not told their children they were separating as they wanted to protect them as long as they could from news which they thought would be devastating. When they finally told their children, however, the children expressed relief at finally having the truth acknowledged. The kids explained that they had sensed something was wrong but not knowing what, they had feared something much worse. Where there is a vacuum, children will imagine and fear the worst. When they are developmentally old enough it is better to be honest and open with them. There are things that children of course do not need to be burdened by, so if in doubt about children's needs in this area it is always wise to speak to a therapist or children's specialist who can help work out where the appropriate line is and the best way to deliver difficult news.

The extent to which parents can manage their own feelings of loss will determine how much they can tolerate and accept the feelings of loss in their children. While it is obvious that children are real people with real feelings, many adults act as if children are deaf — for example, talking as if they were not present or disregarding their feelings about loss and death. It may be a pet that dies or a change of school that involves a loss of friends. These changes can affect children deeply and mindfulness allows sensitivity and compassion rather than glossing over or trivializing children's feelings.

Mindfulness provides a container for whatever is being experienced. It is hard for parents to watch children suffer. No parent wants that. However, by being okay with what is, parents model that suffering can be borne and they give their children the message, 'I am okay, and you are okay.'

CHAPTER 12
Raising mindful children

We have explored the importance of mindful parenting and how this fosters intimacy with our children. We have also explored the importance of parenting in a way that is unified and conscious, in order to maximize the likelihood that children will grow into responsible teenagers and adults. The key to this happening, as we have seen, is for parents to *embody* mindfulness — to *be* the change, as Gandhi would say. In the first part of this chapter we will go into more depth about what it means to truly embody mindfulness. Then we will outline ways of encouraging children to meditate and apply mindfulness informally in their lives so that they can also take responsibility for their own wellbeing.

Embodying mindfulness

We first introduced the notion of embodiment in Chapter 2, where we saw how it is a fundamental part of being mindful. The ability to anchor ourselves in the present moment through our bodies, and to sense what is happening there, allows us to develop intimacy with ourselves.

Only then can we become intimate with other people and the world in general. In a very real sense, intimacy with anyone and anything starts by being in touch with our bodies. In this chapter we will expand this notion of embodiment to also include modelling qualities such as curiosity, non-judgement and compassion to our children. This gives them the opportunity to recognize these qualities in themselves and to start cultivating them in their own lives.

Reflect on a time when you were at your very best as a parent. Chances are you were very present and that there was a sense of genuine connection between you and your child/children. When we are present life is richer and more enjoyable, and relationships simply work better because we are more open to what is happening and therefore slower to judge and react. Of course, just as with mindfulness in general, being present as a parent is relatively easy when we are relaxed and things are going well, but becomes more difficult when we are busy or stressed, or when there is conflict. In these moments we need to practise both recognizing that we are distracted or reactive and simply coming back to the present, over and over.

One way to do this is to treat our interactions with our children as a mindfulness practice. Since mindfulness meditation at its most basic is simply tuning in to what is happening in the senses, it is possible to 'meditate' on our kids. A mindfulness course participant once said that she used to be full of resentment when she had to get out of bed to feed her baby. As much as she recognized that it was not a good thing, she found she would sit there breastfeeding her baby, willing her to go back to sleep so she could return to her own bed, and fighting feelings of resentment. She found this experience distressing as she judged herself harshly for having such thoughts about her child. But about midway through the course she reported having an epiphany. One night she got up as usual for the second or third time and instead of being caught up in resentment she suddenly tuned right in to the feeling of warmth and softness of her daughter, her smell and the soft noises she was making as she fed. She had a moment of spontaneous mindfulness and a sense of connection she had not felt before. From then on she treated each feeding like a mindfulness practice and let herself discover more and more pleasant things that she had previously been oblivious to. Other parents in mindfulness courses or individual therapy have described similar experiences of meditating on their kids — and the benefits they have noticed, both to their own mental health and also to the relationship. It is possible to do this with children of all ages, as well as teenagers and adults. Simply engage your attention with what is actually happening in the senses in any moment, rather than how you would like things to be. Notice the benefits this has for you personally and also for the relationship.

EXERCISE: MEDITATING ON YOUR CHILD/TEENAGER

Set aside some time to spend with your child. You might like to join them in some play activity, climb into bed with them and read them a story or maybe just be close to them. And obviously you can do this while breastfeeding.

Take a moment to check in with yourself and notice if there is any sense of impatience or expectations that things be a certain way. This will show up as tension in the body and mind. If you notice this, begin to let it go. Make sure you don't judge yourself for having it.

Now, tune in to your child. Just as with breath meditation where we tune in to the movement of our breath, here you can choose anything that is happening in the five senses and bring your attention to that. You might, in fact, like to start by noticing your child's breathing. Just take a moment to hear it or watch the expansion and contraction. If you are touching them you may even feel it. Tune in to their warmth and softness, or the sound of their voice or laughter. Try to see what they are seeing — really step into their world and experience it as they are experiencing it.

If you get distracted or impatient simply note that this has happened and re-engage your attention on your child.

Notice the effect this has on your relationship with your child, as well as your own sense of wellbeing (as you slow down and spend more time in the present).

If your child is older, you can do exactly the same thing. You can meditate on them, which helps you discover a fresh perspective, especially if there is any sense of struggle in the relationship. And you can make the commitment to be fully present when you are speaking with them, engaged in some activity or even helping them with their homework. Again, notice the benefits this has on your relationship with them.

You can also just more generally cultivate the intention to be present when around your children. Try this for a day or even an hour and see what effect it has. When you act from an intention to be present with your children you will let go of expectations that things should be a certain way. You will notice that you feel more relaxed and open and have an attitude of curiosity. Children are like sponges and learn mostly through copying what their primary caregivers and other important figures are doing. So quite simply, if you show up in a distracted way, your kids learn to be distracted. But if you show up in a way where you are really present and engaged, they will naturally start to embody these qualities. Having your own regular mindfulness meditation practice, even just a few minutes a day, will help you to do this.

Encouraging children to meditate

As well as cultivating the ability to be mindful in each moment through informal mindfulness practices, it can also be really good for kids to meditate. This is an effective way of improving their wellbeing and resilience, inoculating them against societal and academic pressures that seem to become more intense with every year that passes. It also maximizes the likelihood of a harmonious family life.

The first rule for helping someone establish a regular meditation practice is to have one ourselves. As therapists, both authors know how necessary it is to embody qualities of mindfulness and also to be able to respond to questions about mindfulness from a place of experience rather than just some concept we read in a book. Nobody can effectively teach mindfulness if they don't have their own regular practice. So, as a first step, we should get our own practice going. This helps us to experience strategies that support regular practice, as well as common obstacles that can get in the way when our kids start out. Also, we all know how kids respond to people telling them to do one thing while themselves doing another. You might like to refer back to page 45 for tips on establishing a regular practice for yourself.

Really, the same principles apply as for adults. In brief, these are:
- Start small. Aim for five minutes twice a day to start with and increase this once a routine has been established.
- As a general rule, bookend the day with meditation: that is,

meditate first thing in the morning to start the day with mindfulness and then again at the end of the day. If your schedule allows, it can be good to pause in the middle of the day to meditate. You can be flexible and see what works best for you and your kids.

- Use resources like apps, MP3s and other resources — especially ones designed for kids such as Smiling Mind.

- Treat the whole thing like an experiment; be curious, notice what supports the practice and what obstacles arise. Then do more of what works and find creative options to manage any difficulties. You might need to find a space in the home that is just for meditation at certain times of the day or come up with new rules around technology so as there is time for meditation. When you are curious as to what works and what doesn't you will bring more relaxation into the whole experience rather than making it another thing to fit into the family schedule.

- Notice the benefits of meditating as this will provide intrinsic motivation to continue.

- If for whatever reason you stop meditating for a time, just begin again as soon as you notice this has happened. In this way, it makes no difference whether you get lost in default mode for 30 seconds (as in when we are meditating) or three weeks. You just start again whenever you realize.

- And it also helps to remember that the goal is not to stop the thoughts from happening. Thinking is inevitable. But with mindfulness we get better at recognizing when the mind has wandered and therefore faster at bringing it back. So we don't stop thinking but we do stop getting lost in our thoughts. This is a very important distinction and one that should be made clear to children when they start out.

- Finally, meditating *with* our kids has a number of benefits such as implicit encouragement and sharing the experience with them. Initially they may want you to be there, and as they get older or more comfortable with the practice they may prefer to do it on their own.

Here are some suggestions for mindfulness practices that you can try with your kids:

- *Simple breath meditation*: Set aside a few minutes and sit with your kids. Focus on the breath, as we have explored already in this book.

- *Balloon breathing*: To capitalize on children's natural creativity and imagination, you might like to get them to imagine a balloon in their belly as they breathe. They can notice how it expands and contracts. Ask them what colour their balloon is, or even whether it changes colour as they breathe in and out.

- *Rocking*: Make an origami boat following simple online instructions or get your child's favourite soft toy. Ask them to lie down and place the boat or toy on their belly and notice how it rocks as they breathe. They can imagine the boat is rocking over waves or that they are rocking the toy to sleep.

- *Guessing by feel*: Take your child outside. Both of you go and find three or four items (e.g. leaves, pine cones, rocks) without showing the other person. Then ask your child to close their eyes, and place each item into their hand, one by one. Ask them to describe what it feels like. What do they find interesting about it? See if they can guess what it is just using touch. Then switch roles.

- *Mindful colouring*: Give your child some colouring in to do and encourage them to really pay attention. Explore the use of colour and ask them how different colours make them feel in their body. If they are old enough, encourage them to stay within the lines. And just to ensure this doesn't become an exercise in perfectionism, also make sure you encourage them to intentionally, consciously go outside the lines! Explore with them what it feels like to do this.

- *Big/small*: Stand in front of your child and take a few moments to sense the breath together. Breathe in and out at the same time. Then, when inhaling, allow the body to expand (e.g. arms out, standing tall). Get bigger and bigger as the breath comes in. Then exhale and get progressively smaller, until at the end of the exhalation you are both curled up as small as possible.

- *Trees/seaweed*: Stand in front of your child, close to them, and ask them to close their eyes. Blow gently on them and get them to move 'in the wind' as a tree would. See if they can make big wiggling, waving movements when you blow hard and smaller movements as your breath softens toward the end of the exhalation. Alternatively, you can both stand with your eyes open and be seaweed together, wiggling in the current. Imagine that the current starts out strong and you both move a lot. Then as you imagine the current getting softer you can both move less and less. In both exercises, the object is to come to a state of stillness at the end. You might like to just stand and breathe together, feeling your feet on the floor. This is a great exercise for children who have difficulty keeping still.

Any activity can become a mindfulness practice simply by emphasizing connection with the senses. If your children (of any age) have a favourite game, think about how you could weave mindfulness into it. For instance, if they like hide-and-seek, how quiet can they be? There are even games like 'dead fish' and 'statues' where the object is to remain completely still. Or when driving, you can play 'I-spy' or just look out for cars of a specific colour. Get creative and adapt what you are already doing into a mindfulness exercise.

Raising responsible citizens

The foundation of ethics is being present and aware. While we could write a whole book on this enormous topic alone, in this section we outline some basic ways to teach kids to use the qualities they cultivate in mindfulness practice to strengthen their moral compass and to live more meaningful, responsible lives.

Have you ever realized that it is impossible to take something that doesn't belong to you without first generating a whole lot of greed in your mind? Or that to swat a mosquito you must first generate anger? Often, in the busyness of life, we fail to notice this. And this is not helped by how busy our minds tend to become in response to the frantic pace of modern life. But if we slow down and really check things out, we will see that this is true. Next time you go to kill something, pause for a moment and notice the angry thoughts and the general sense of malice and ill-will. And notice the suffering that accompanies these mental states. We generally know that when we are consumed with rage or some other afflictive emotion it is a very uncomfortable experience. But what is harder to notice is that even the smallest amount of such emotions causes tension and contraction in our body.

In the same way, helping kids to recognize the suffering that comes with negative actions such as stealing and lying — and the pleasant feelings that come with positive actions such as generosity and helping others — is an extremely important step in raising ethical, responsible human beings. If children are caught out in a lie, for instance, it can be a good idea to sit with them and help them explore why they felt it necessary to lie, and also to help them recognize how this creates unpleasant sensations in their body and confusion in their mind. If they steal, it can be good to explore with them the greed that grips their body and mind, as well as how the person they stole from might feel — if they are at a developmental stage where such empathy is possible for them, of course.

What most supports having conversations like this is to embody non-judgement and openness. When we meditate the goal is to open ourselves to what is there without judging it or trying to control it. And good mindfulness teachers always maintain the intention to bring this non-judgemental attitude to any exploration of what comes up in the group or therapy session. In the same way, embodying this sense when we discuss things with others means that they are less likely to get defensive or feel the need to try to hide or distort things. This then creates a clearing for an honest conversation where both parties can be heard and where there is a chance of real insight taking place. Always come back to what *is* — to the reality of the tension in the mind and body that comes with unethical behaviour. This is far more powerful than a moral lecture.

EXERCISE: USING OUR BODY TO GUIDE OUR BEHAVIOUR

As a first step, become familiar with the process of self-inquiry yourself. Then you will be able to help your children use it to explore the effects of their own behaviour.

Take a moment to close your eyes and sense your way into your body. Notice your breath. Become aware of tension and begin to let it go. Notice without judgement any sensations present in your body right now. Take your awareness deeper and notice any feelings and emotions that are around. Allow everything to be exactly as it is.

If you notice any emotions that feel as if they are reactions (resentment, anxiety, anger etc.) sit with them for a while and make space for them. It can help to name them, to breathe with them and to soften around them by letting go of any tension. It can also be very powerful to give yourself permission to have them, recognizing that they are normal human emotions.

Practising this regularly will make it possible to inquire into your emotional state at other times throughout the day — 'off the cushion', so to speak. And once you become able to do this you can start being curious about the effects different behaviours, thoughts and beliefs have on you, just by inquiring into your body whenever they are present.

And when you sense any tension or unpleasant sensations it is likely that you are resisting something or doing something that lacks integrity for you on a deep level. Having noticed this tension, you can start inquiring into what that is. In this way, physical tension becomes a sort of early warning indicator that something is not sitting well with you.

Once you have become familiar with doing this process yourself, you can start to invite your children to be interested with what is happening in their bodies when they act in unethical ways. Helping them to realize that these actions harm them as well as others — by producing tension and unpleasant sensations in their bodies — can be a powerful lesson to give to them.

And on the other side of the coin, of course, is ethical behaviour. As we have already said, when we act in ways that have integrity and benefit others, we tend to relax and experience pleasant emotions such as joy. Helping children to recognize this, and taking time to savour and amplify the experience, makes it more likely they will act in similarly ethical ways in the future.

Because our brain acts like Velcro for negative experiences and Teflon for positive — that is, the negative sticks while the positive slides away — it is good to both practise and teach children to 'take in the good'. This is a phrase coined by neuropsychologist Rick Hanson, who writes about how we can build inner strengths by overwriting the brain's default setting via consciously focusing on pleasant experiences and body sensations and spending time savouring these. This could be enjoying a chocolate or watching a sunset. When we focus on a positive experience for ten seconds or more, it gets hardwired into our nervous system. We are then more likely to notice subsequent positive experiences, as well as being able to recall them afterward. In this way, we literally rewire our brain for happiness. It is very useful to teach children to do this.

EXERCISE: SAVOURING (AND HARDWIRING) POSITIVE EXPERIENCES

Look around you and notice what the most pleasant thing is about the situation you are currently in. Perhaps you are doing something you enjoy. Or perhaps there is a pleasant sight or sound you notice when you take the time to look and listen.

Focus on this pleasant experience and notice how it feels in your body. Really let yourself enjoy the pleasant feelings. Let positive thoughts fill your mind. Spend at least ten seconds (more if you like) enjoying the experience. Let it permeate your whole being.

For the rest of the day, any time you notice a pleasant experience — or if you complete something you have been meaning to complete, such as sending an email — savour the pleasant experience or sense of accomplishment. Notice the effect this has on your day.

Most parents know that taking time to celebrate their children's successes and good behaviour is both reinforcing of the behaviour itself as well as simply being a pleasant way to connect with their kids. So when kids connect to the feeling inside themselves when they are acting in integrity they learn to want more of this intrinsically.

CHAPTER 13

Creating a mindful family

There's no place like home, there's no place like home …
Dorothy, *The Wizard of Oz*

Once we have become intimate with ourselves, our partner and our children, we can let this ripple out even further. We can use mindfulness to create a family culture and environment that feels inclusive and safe, and reflects our family values. This is more than how we are as parents. It is about how mindfulness can help us discover more intimacy in our home and make our family feel like a haven. Having a heartfelt, genuine sense of intimacy with our family is profound. It creates a security and a sense of being known and appreciated for who we are. When we are at home with who we are and we don't need to hide away the vulnerable bits, we set a tone for our family that is also accepting. Centrally the message is: all of you is welcome here. Fundamentally we all need to belong. It is one thing to know conceptually that we are part of a family; it is another thing entirely to sense this connection in the depths of our being. And the family is what gives or doesn't give this sense of wellbeing, acceptance and belonging. If there is an atmosphere of warmth and calm in the home this is palpable. It creates a clearing for the happiness and healthy development we are talking about throughout *Mindful Relationships.* This chapter is about considering our families through the lens of mindfulness to bring more awareness and effective functioning into our homes.

The family unit is the building block for society as a whole, and as such, mindful families are central to the achievement of peace and to building a mindful world. And it starts with feeling at home in ourselves. When we develop the clear-seeing that comes from a mindfulness practice, we begin to see both the joy and the pain within our families. And when we hold this with loving presence, we become agents of change. We forgive ourselves for our mistakes and act to change what needs to be changed. Mindfulness helps us develop these skills.

The family as a container for development

Families come in all shapes and sizes. They are bound together by blood, marriage and name. We are all socialized into families. Many factors shape our own particular version of family and in turn influence the development of family members. These might be the same factors that influenced our parents. Or they could be factors such as different racial customs and traditions, attitudes to socializing or work, contributing to society, beliefs about religion or class — the list is endless. The family is the container that shapes our self-worth and our experience of relating to the wider world. It is shaped by the way we communicate and the rules we live by.

There are rules in every family that operate to define our sense of belonging and connection. We learn where the line is — what behaviours, thoughts or feelings are okay and what is likely to be rejected. There are messages we receive about our self-worth and about communication in the family. For example, we learn what is safe to say and what cannot be spoken about. Sometimes the rules are conscious but more often they are just absorbed. The family is the container in which we absorb these rules. Most of the time it is assumed that the rules are known and understood by all members but often this is not the case. A good metaphor for family life is that of an iceberg. Members are aware of a tiny proportion of what is going on, the bits that they see and hear. They often know that there is more but they may have no idea how to find out what is going on beneath the surface. The family's emotional wellbeing depends on understanding the needs below the surface of everyday family events just as the captain of a ship needs to know the extent of the iceberg to determine which direction to sail in.

Mindfulness facilitates new awareness, new consciousness and new learnings. When the family is open to changing its communication patterns, habits, culture or rules there is the potential for a new vitality and joy to bubble up. It's not that people don't have fights or difficulties, but rather that people can take risks, make mistakes, say what they think and express affection and emotion. In such a family there is a lot of energy, life and comfort. The family can trust their relationships and because of this they can disagree without it being a disaster. The home is for living in and not for a *Vogue* magazine shoot. Think about this for a moment. Pause and consider what the feeling is like in your family. Is it generally friendly and enjoyable or is it cold and dead, or overly polite, secretive or confusing? In a less mindful family, rules are rigid and do not adapt to meet the growth of the members and people are scared to say what they think for fear of being shamed, bullied or criticized.

EXERCISE: KNOWING YOUR FAMILY

Think about what defines your family and the extent to which members feel they belong. Is there a black sheep? You might like to discuss this with your family members. The idea is to get people to reflect and share both the positive and negative feelings they have about the family rules and to be open to exploring what is working and what is not. Obviously you need to adapt the conversation to the age of the children but when members feel they have a say they begin to take more ownership and can also feel more deeply connected in the family.

The following questions can guide the exploration: What does it feel like for you being in this family? What do you like/dislike about our family? What defines us as a family? Do you feel included/ excluded in our family? Why?

Children get attention by taking a position in the family that is often different from that of their siblings. They attempt to carve out a unique path for themselves. For example, if one person is serious and hard-working, another may have taken on the role of the clown. Or if one is very responsible another might have become used to expecting to be taken care of. Mindfulness helps us have effective conversations about this so we can more easily see the roles that we and other family members have taken on. When we sense inwards and notice the sensations in our body of tension or relaxation, when we become aware of our beliefs about our worthiness and the self-judgements we make and learn to hold this with friendliness and compassion, we open up to more genuine presence. When we can be with our vulnerability we can look directly at family members, not through one another, and we can speak with clear voices and relaxed facial expressions. We can speak directly to people rather than via a third person. Living in a family like this means we do not avoid each other by getting lost in work, nor do we cover up our pain or our joy.

Family culture

Family culture can be defined as 'the spirit or feeling that grows out of the collective patterns of behaviour that characterize family interaction. And these things, like the tip of the iceberg, come out of the mass of shared beliefs and values underneath.'[1] Mindfulness makes us more aware of the beliefs, values, thoughts and actions that influence family culture.

The foundation of a good family culture is awareness. By sensing into how each member feels in the family we can begin to develop the capacity for more conscious choices in the family. In thinking about our family and the culture we wish to create, we might begin by having an open conversation similar to the exercise above. We might invite members to talk about family values and culture. Mindfulness facilitates this by helping us to communicate effectively, without judgement or blame, allowing space for everyone's feelings, and bringing an attitude of friendliness to each family member. When we are able to have open, honest conversations like these we can start consciously choosing rules and expectations that function well. Again, as with our relationships, we are going to have a family culture so we might as well create it consciously. We can do more of what works and less of what doesn't, and each family member has a voice in this process.

When reflecting on the family culture we hope to create, it helps to think about our motivation. In healthy families, members relate to one another with compassion and love, rather than just being out for themselves. Focusing on the 'we' rather than the 'I' can mean the difference between wellness and illness. It means that people feel happy when they see others happy. This strengthens the family culture. Deliberately cultivating loving presence with mindfulness and allowing this to radiate out to people in our family helps create the possibility of this. Mindfulness *is* love in action. It is not just a feeling but it becomes the ground that fertilizes all we do in family life. But if we want a deep transformation in our family, it takes practice. Otherwise, our habitual patterns and need for comfort will override our best intentions.

EXERCISE: SENSING YOUR DEEPEST LONGING FOR YOUR FAMILY

Try meditating for a few minutes and sensing the quality of your family relationships. Are they tender, warm and close or is there conflict and distance? You might like to write in a journal about what you discover.

Then inquire into what your deepest longing for your family is. Keep asking the question, 'What really matters in my family?'

It might be helpful to do this exercise a number of times, noting how it changes over time.

Once we have got in touch with our deepest longing for our family, we may start to recognize various patterns we have that get in the way of this. The following exercise can help us to use mindfulness to see clearly what these patterns are and to change them.

EXERCISE: ACCESSING YOUR WISDOM TO CHANGE YOUR PATTERNS

Bring to mind a time at home with a family member where you know you are reactive. What is the recurring pattern? Is it a need to be right? Or are you critical and judgemental?

Try watching this as you would watch a movie and press pause at the point when you get stuck in reactivity. Go through frame by frame and see if you can notice the actual judgements and reactions that get you stuck. Bring a non-judgemental awareness to this.

Next, get in touch with a sense of loving presence. We have discussed how to do this throughout the book. It can help to bring to mind a person or figure that connects you with this sense. For some people this is a loving family member. For others it could be nature or some special place. Others might bring to mind Jesus or Buddha or some other figure that connects them with a sense of universal love and wisdom. Notice how this feels in your body, mind and heart.

Now, bring this wisdom and love back to the scene of conflict. How would you like to be? What is possible for you now in responding to this person/situation that you didn't see before? What is possible when you choose love, compassion and friendliness over being right? Keep coming back and sensing what is most truthful for you about your aspiration. Remember, mindfulness is about using our bodies and our senses.

As well as getting in touch with our deepest longing and allowing wisdom to change family culture, there are a number of simple, practical ways of creating more mindful families. These are offered in the exercise on the following page.

EXERCISES: TIPS FOR CREATING MINDFUL FAMILIES

Making mindful transitions

When you arrive home carrying the stress and worry of the day, park your car down the street and take ten minutes to meditate or relax and let go of the day so you can be aware of the quality of presence and energy you bring into your home. Between the stimulus and response is the pause. Otherwise it is all reactivity.

Reunions and departures

Take note of how well you separate and come together again in your family and see what you value or what you would like to do differently here. Pay attention to being present as opposed to ignoring people when they come home and leave again.

Seeing the best in each family member

Bring a loved one to mind right now and imagine what it would be like to relate to him/her without judgement or reactivity. Try to really connect to their essential nature and appreciate who they are without ego. What does it feel like? Breathe in deeply now from a place of loving and openness and hold this person in this way in your heart. Now, remind yourself of the transience of life and know that at any time it could all change. We are mortal and life is essentially out of our control. Let both the experience of open-heartedness and the realization of impermanence permeate your being.

Having a mindful intention

When you are in a tricky communication pattern choose the intention you hope to have for the end of the discussion. Some examples are 'I intend to understand you', 'I intend to listen well', 'I intend to be really present for you', 'I intend to bring you love' or 'I intend to send you love'.

Choosing acceptance

When you notice the blame or criticism stories coming up, practise catching yourself and notice what happens when you say inwardly, 'I accept him/her completely as they are.' Having this intention is likely to make the other person less reactive even if you don't explicitly state it.

Mindful hugs

Create relaxation and increase closeness and bonding. Hug and hold members of your family regularly without expecting anything but just to give them love. Really allow yourself to be present and sense into the experience of holding and being held.

Mindful listening

Explore how you can foster listening in your family: brainstorm dinner table conversations, bedtime rituals, listening during conflict.

Mindful talking

Awareness of the power of the words we use and their effect on others comes as we increase in awareness generally by practising mindfulness. Have an intention to speak directly to the person involved in any issue and not to speak about family members behind their backs.

The smile down

Take a breath and sense what it is like right now to let go and imagine a vast sky that is smiling down and descending on your family. Let that smile filter through your whole body. Now feel that the smile extends from inside of you into each member of your family. Visualize this smile floating into each person and also in between them. Sense the whole of your family living within this smile. Let the smile begin to radiate out from family members into the home environment and flow into the spaces of your home. Imagine that your entire family is held and encircled by this wide open smile. Let the smile be the container. Sense into living a question of what is possible for your family and let go of any anxiety or tension that you might be inclined to have about the family.

The more we practise mindfulness the more we intuitively know the right course of action and behaviours in circumstances of difficulty. We learn to forgive quickly and apologize wholeheartedly, we learn when kindness is needed and we learn the importance of being trustworthy and of keeping our agreements. Mindfulness develops our capacity to look with compassion on others and decrease the sense of separation.

Managing use of technology

We are born with an innate curiosity. Watch little kids and you will see them interact with their world through their senses, fascinated by insects and leaves and dirt. They are naturally in the moment a lot of the time, seemingly effortlessly. As we age, however, life becomes busier. We start to take things for granted and do them on autopilot, with our attention elsewhere. We also start to relate to the world through concepts and ideas instead of experiencing it directly through the senses. As we do this, we start to lose touch with our natural curiosity. The good news is that it is innate and we never actually lose it — we just lose touch with it. And, as we have seen throughout *Mindful Relationships*, we can reconnect with it if we cultivate it by once again relating to the world more through our senses rather than just through concepts.

Technology is neither good nor bad. Just as the power of nuclear fission and fusion can be used for great good or great harm, so too with all other forms of technology. Digital technology — television, computers, the internet and personal electronic devices — is exactly the same. It is how it is used that determines whether it benefits or harms us.

Television

Television can be a great source of entertainment and information if watched in moderation. However, the amount of TV we watch has increased significantly in recent years.[2] Excessive amounts (more than one hour per day for kids and two for adults) have been found to lead to a range of problems such as obesity, sleep disruption, behavioural problems and aggression, impaired academic performance and reduced creative play.[3] Watching TV as a child can cause attentional problems, especially watching fast-paced cartoons.[4] In one study, just nine minutes of viewing *SpongeBob SquarePants* was enough to temporarily reduce children's ability to plan and delay gratification, and sustained viewing over time can create lasting changes.[5] Indeed, each hour of television viewing increases by 1.3 times the risk of later going on to develop Alzheimer's disease.[6]

Electronic devices

Smartphones, tablets and other devices have the ability to add a great deal to our lives. Being able to look up information, shop and communicate via Skype with loved ones around the world is quite an incredible thing and is fundamentally transforming and enriching our lives. Unfortunately, these same devices tend to encourage distractibility and reactivity. The default setting in devices and apps is for alerts to be on, meaning that we are constantly interrupted in the middle of one activity and invited — we might say enticed — to switch our attention to another. This trains us to jump from one thing to another rather than focusing on one thing at a time. This then makes it hard for us to sustain attentional focus on tasks such as work and study, or conversations at the dinner table. Sadly, there is an increasing tendency to use technology at the dinner table and in social situations generally. It is not uncommon to see a couple dining out where one or both are on their phones. Young people travelling on public transport often sit glued to their screens instead of interacting with the people around them. And there is a prevailing — although completely erroneous — belief that it is possible to hold a conversation while simultaneously texting or using devices.

Research has also found that up to 25 per cent of young people are actually addicted to their phones. They demonstrate all the characteristic symptoms of addiction such as increased tolerance, withdrawal, inability to change their behaviour and impaired relationships with peers, as well as a reduced sense of fulfilment in peer relationships.[7,8]

But it is not just young people. Recent surveys have indicated that around 57 per cent of people check work emails while on family outings and 38 per cent routinely check work emails at the dinner table.[9] This tendency leads to personal stress and missed opportunities for connection with family members. It also sends a terrible message to young people, who tend to model a lot of their behaviour from their parents. This tendency is only likely to get worse in the future as we become even more accustomed to technology being a central part of our working and personal lives, and become habituated to things such as smartphones at the table and talking to people who are simultaneously having a number of other conversations. Well, trying to, anyway.

Overuse of technology creates other problems that extend beyond social issues. Research by Michael Gradisar in 2011 found that nine out of ten Americans used digital technology, such as watching TV or using their phone, in the hour before going to bed. The light emitted by these devices can disrupt normal sleep–wake cycles and impair sleep quality.[9] Furthermore, people who reported using more interactive devices, such as smartphones (compared to the relatively more passive television viewing) had more difficulties falling asleep and also reported not feeling refreshed in the morning.[10]

Mindful use of technology

So how do we counter these disturbing trends? At a very minimum, it might be a good idea to have rules around smartphones being put away at mealtimes. People in our courses have told us that when they go out to dinner with friends, everyone puts their phone face-down in the middle of the table and the first person to check theirs picks up the tab. This is a fun way of ensuring people actually connect with each other when they are socializing.

It is also a good idea to limit use of technology generally in the home. Television and other electronic devices are an important part of modern life and it is probably not a good idea to try to prevent children from accessing them at all, but responsible, aware use should be modelled and encouraged by parents. The American Academy of Pediatrics discourage media use by children younger than two and recommend limiting screen time to no more than one or two hours a day for children and teens, and banning screens of any type in children's bedrooms.[11]

It really is up to parents to model intelligent use of technology. Just as being mindful and attentive with children and teenagers models this behaviour and makes it more likely that they themselves will be mindful, using technology with awareness will encourage this behaviour. Switch it off when having conversations and ensure that you engage in technology-free downtime before bed. Read a book, meditate and find other ways to wind down. When children see their parents doing this, they are more likely to do it themselves — particularly when there are strict boundaries in place around technology use. It can also be useful to have conversations with children around what they post online, to avoid them exposing themselves or reactively posting statements or updates in the heat of the moment that they might regret later. In some ways this is the new 'birds and the bees' talk. Most schools now offer training in this for young people and parents, but it can be good to establish open lines of communication about these things in the home, so that children trust they can come to their parents if they are being bullied or are unsure about whether their technology use is safe or problematic. This might take the form of an informal conversation with your children where you outline guidelines for intelligent, conscious use. However, in cases where children are exhibiting the features of addiction discussed earlier, it might be necessary to establish and enforce strict structures around how technology is used by all family members.

PART 5

The mindful workplace

CHAPTER 14

Working mindfully

There is a prevailing mentality that we should be able to multitask. Somehow over the past three decades or so the assumption has become that effective workers are able to do five or ten things at once and that we should be constantly connected to each other via the internet and smartphones. And that this is the secret to productivity. But as we will see in this chapter, multitasking is actually an illusion, and trying to do it leads to increased stress. This stress in turn reduces our efficiency and also impairs communication, with the result that our work relationships suffer. Being connected 24/7 produces the same problems, and there is increasingly a move away from this in large tech companies.

We will explore how doing one thing at a time paradoxically means that we get more done, with less stress and greater work satisfaction. Just in case all of this sounds rather counterintuitive, we promise that it will all make sense by the end of the chapter!

The myth of multitasking

Here's a simple fact: the human brain processes information serially, not parallel. That is, it processes information one piece at a time and is simply incapable of processing two or more complex things simultaneously. For instance, if you are driving your car while talking on your phone, your attention is rapidly cycling between the driving and the conversation. It switches back and forth so fast that it *seems* as if you are doing both at once, but you are not. This is why if you are deep in the conversation and something takes place on the road ahead, your reaction time is slowed. Conversely, if we are making a turn in busy traffic, we will not be focused on the phone call and might have to ask the caller to repeat what they just said. Research indicates that we are four times more likely to crash within five minutes of talking on the phone, and that it is the equivalent to having a blood alcohol content of 0.08 per cent (i.e. nearly twice the legal limit in many parts of the world).[1] Research also shows that if we are texting or using the internet on our phone while driving, we are a whopping 164 times more likely to crash.[2] This is why doing so is now illegal in many places in the world.

A great experiment to illustrate this involves getting people to get into pairs and asking one to speak about something they are passionate about while the other listens. Simultaneously, the listener is instructed to send texts or check social media on their phone. What becomes apparent is that the listener's attention cycles between each task rather than being able to focus on both at once. This impairs their ability to catch what is being said. It also significantly reduces the quality of the interaction, with both speaker and listener feeling disconnected.

What people also notice in this experiment is that each time they switch their attention from one thing to another, there is a brief pause where they are not paying attention to anything at all. Called the 'attentional blink', this phenomenon has mainly been studied in terms of visual information but occurs whenever we switch our attentional focus. The attentional systems in the brain go offline (technically, this is called a refractory period) for between 200 and 500 milliseconds (that is, up to half a second).[3] During this time we are not paying attention to anything at all, and will miss any information that is presented to us. The more stressed we are, the longer the blink, by the way. So for half a second, it is as if we are not even there. The following brief exercise brings this to life.

EXERCISE: NOTICING THE ATTENTIONAL BLINK

Repeat to yourself, silently, the letters A to Z as fast as you can.

Now the numbers 1 to 26.

Now, very simply switch between letters and numbers: A1, B2, C3 … all the way to Z26.

Notice what happens as you do this.

During the experiment, you would have noticed a very obvious slowing down. That's the attentional blink. You probably also lost track, somewhere around D4 (or E5 if you are really good). This is happening all the time although we generally don't notice it. It is just going on in the background. But the implications are significant. Obviously, if we are trying to 'multitask' while we are communicating we miss important information and the quality of the relationship suffers. But the implications go beyond communication. So many people, having bought into the 'multitasking mentality', work and study in this way, constantly switching their attention from one thing to another, for instance from their work to Facebook to email, to Instagram, to their phone — all the while with music or TV on in the background. And since each time we switch our attention we lose half a second, this starts to add up. Do that 120 times and we lose a minute. That's not a minute spent on Facebook while we should be working, but a minute lost getting from our work *to* Facebook and back again. Research also shows that when we check an email, it takes an average of 64 seconds to get our attention fully back to what we were doing before.[4] Which means if we do that every five minutes in a typical 40-hour working week, we waste *eight and a half hours*. So doing this is clearly a recipe for inefficiency.

In addition, a small pilot study conducted by Hewlett-Packard in 2005 found that workers who were constantly distracted in this way actually experienced a measurable reduction in their IQ that was twice as bad as if they had been smoking marijuana.[5] These kinds of findings have led Clifford Nash, a researcher from Stanford and an expert in 'multitasking', to conclude that:

> *[People] … doing five, six or more things at once all the*
> *time … are terrible at every aspect of multitasking! They get*
> *distracted constantly. Their memory is very disorganized. Recent*
> *work we've done suggests that they're worse at analytical*
> *reasoning. We worry that we may be creating people who may*
> *not be able to think well, or clearly.*[6]

Being constantly bombarded with information and trying to 'multitask' in hyperkinetic workplaces also increases stress, which further impairs performance by compromising executive functioning, particularly short-term memory and attention regulation.[7,8,9]

Furthermore, the cortisol released during stress responses impairs our ability to absorb new information and connect emotionally with others, further reducing work performance.[10]

Edward Hallowell, a US psychiatrist who taught at the Harvard Medical School for twenty years, has even identified an emerging phenomenon he terms 'Attention Deficit Trait' (ADT). Unlike ADHD, which is an interaction of genetic and environmental factors, ADT is purely environmental. In essence, it is a chronic fight/flight response, where the brain is hijacked by the amygdala. According to Hallowell, it results in black and white thinking; difficulty staying organized, setting priorities and managing time; and a pervasive sense of mild panic and guilt.

Learning to unitask

The solution to all of this, obviously, is to focus on one thing at a time. There are two ways to do this, as outlined in the exercise below.

EXERCISE: LEARNING TO UNITASK

Method one: Focusing on one thing at a time

Make a list of things that need to be done, prioritize them and then focus on one task at a time until that task is completed.

When you have completed it, take a moment to enjoy (savour) the experience of completion before moving on to the next task.

For example, if you are writing an email and the phone rings, you could simply let the phone go to voicemail and check the message later, after the email is sent.

Method two: Efficient attention switching

If you have the kind of job where you need to switch your attention between tasks — for instance, a physician in an emergency department gets interrupted an average of 50 times per hour with life-threatening situations — you might need to switch attentional focus. But the goal here is to do it as little as possible and give your full attention to one task at a time.

To return to our example, if the call was important you might answer the phone. But if so then completely let go of the email rather than trying to finish it while having a distracted conversation. In this case, the email becomes the distraction, and the mindfulness practice is to return the attention to the call every time it gets hooked up in the email once again.

Turning off alerts on our computers and devices supports unitasking. Rather than being interrupted constantly while we are trying to focus, with enticing invitations to switch our attention to something new, we can remain focused on single tasks for longer periods. A growing number of business coaches also advocate *not* checking email first thing in the morning, as this sets up a reactive pattern for the rest of the day and makes it harder to focus. Instead, it may be better to start the day checking our calendars and prioritizing tasks, even getting started on some of them, and then checking email mid-morning. Some people have even started using automated email responders or including a statement in their signature that they check their emails twice a day — say at 11 am and 3 pm — and inviting people to call if the issue is urgent.

Research shows that mindfulness generally, and unitasking in particular, results in improved performance.[11] Specifically, unitasking leads to better concentration and memory, less biased thinking and improved ability to detect and correct errors.[12,13,14] Focusing on one thing at a time also helps minimize emotional reactions and can even prevent burnout.[15,16]

Decision-making

Learning to focus also has obvious benefits for making better decisions. At its most basic, when we are unfocused we tend to make more mistakes, whether these be dropping plates or agreeing to do things we don't want to. When we are unaware of our mental processes we also become subject to biases in our thinking that can lead to problems. Confirmation biases and anchoring biases are two of the most common. Confirmation biases refer to unconsciously deciding on something and then interpreting new information to confirm what we already know. Or think we know. Anchoring biases refer to neglecting to adapt to new information suggesting alternate possibilities.

Both biases lead to impaired decision-making and are examples of what are referred to as fixed mindsets. Remaining mindfully aware of our thoughts and decision-making processes helps us both notice biases as they arise and correct them. Cultivating open mindsets — what is sometimes referred to as a 'beginner's mind', where there are infinite possibilities, like the experience of a child looking at the ocean for the first time — leads to much more flexibility in thinking and better decision-making.[17]

The importance of downtime

Taking sufficient downtime is crucial to effective performance. Going outside (or at least leaving your desk) at lunchtime, unplugging from the grid after hours, taking vacations or even just taking a moment to pause between tasks helps the body and mind stay relaxed and efficient. Volkswagen experimented a few years ago with turning off their email servers overnight and found that employees who were unable to easily email one another overnight — and therefore actually spent time with their family and got a good night's sleep — became so much more efficient the next day that their overall productivity increased significantly. This was so successful that the policy has now become German labour law. And this from a nation famed for its efficiency.

In order to ensure that we give ourselves enough downtime throughout the day and overnight we can start by taking moments to pause. Doing this disrupts the default mode of rushing from one thing to another and brings a modicum of mindfulness into whatever we are doing. We become more aware of stress and tension in our bodies and minds, which empowers us to take better care of ourselves. And finally, self-compassion makes it much more likely that we will work in ways that are sustainable and kind to ourselves, rather than red-lining all the time and ultimately burning ourselves out.

CHAPTER 15
Mindfulness at work and in groups

Throughout the book we have seen that mindfulness helps us be present, calm and open. In the workplace these traits contribute to a sense of professionalism, responsibility and effective leadership. When we are present and open, we access the possibility of more creative solutions and we get better results. In this chapter we outline some essential principles that can be used at work or equally when in groups to bring about more mindful and harmonious relationships.

When we consider our position within the workplace it's worth considering the workplace culture. A mindful workplace culture is open to change, is flexible and supports the truth. As with families, a workplace culture that is secretive and rigid tends to make people feel confused and oppressed by the unstated and unknown. Contrary to this, a mindful workplace culture is founded on respect for the individuals within it. This creates an atmosphere infused with genuine warmth rather than one dominated by a sense of coldness or hostility.

Conflict resolution

When it comes to conflict resolution we all know that we don't always get what we want, even when we are convinced of our own reasonableness. How we look at a person or situation is influenced by our own perceptions, which are of course always subjective. We may even find ourselves saying things like, 'They just can't seem to … they should have tried harder to … they ought to be more … they never … they always … if only they would make an effort to …'.

These expectations often lead to conflict and it helps if we catch ourselves when we get caught up in them, then let go of the judgements. When we name the feelings that we sense into and acknowledge the pain of those feelings, we can also let them pass through us. A good metaphor is the ocean: the waves come and go but the ocean remains. Similarly our feelings come and go but the idea is that we are not so identified with our feelings that we cannot let them go. When we do this, we are able to navigate our way more skilfully through difficulties and we become more assertive. As well as this, if we are able to hold our experience with loving compassion we may start to recognize the unmet needs that underlie our negative reactions.

Win–win

A good starting point is the idea of win–win. We saw earlier in the book that health is predicated on 'I' coming to include the 'we'. As illness becomes wellness when we include another in relationships, so too win–win works to benefit everyone. A society and a workplace that fosters competition and individual success works against this. There are definite winners and losers. By contrast the attitude of win–win makes for more collaborative workplaces and the result is a synergy and a greater level of happiness and wellbeing all round.

Win–win does not work if we just pretend we are operating from this stance. To negotiate a win–win result means we need to be sincere and genuine in our attempts. It might mean articulating something along the lines of 'I want us both to feel happy with the result here and from my perspective it is not okay for me to get what I want without you also getting what you want'. This ability to be open to compromise is aided by the emotional support that mindfulness provides. We remember to pause, look deeply and try to see clearly. We sense how we feel about a situation, taking note of our bodily sensations and noticing our thoughts — what our judgements are about the situation or the person. We might say, 'I'm sorry that this situation is unacceptable to me (or to you). Can we try to find a solution that works better for both of us?' It generates the possibility of more options. When we can trust our ability to communicate assertively we do not need to go down the path of catastrophizing. The relationship is still fundamentally okay and provides the container in which we can navigate and manage any differences. We can come back to rely on our fundamental relationship knowing that the win–win stance makes it safe. We can trust that we will be heard and understood, which works to reduce our reactivity and this allows us to be collaborative in our workplace relationships.

In modern workplaces we are increasingly expected to do more with fewer resources. To help with this, a mindful employee might say, 'I understand that there are now fewer people to do the same job. But I am feeling too stressed and anxious by the increased demands and I feel I cannot work to the same standard as I have been because of this.' The employee would listen to the response and check for any incorrect assumptions. Then, coming from a stance of win–win, they might say, 'Please help me understand what steps are being taken to help us all manage better as a team as I cannot continue working under this pressure.'

The key here is not to make anyone wrong while at the same time being clear about what our needs are. Mindfulness helps as we can let go of judgements and address the situation as it is. It helps us check whether our perceptions are accurate while stating clearly what is acceptable to us. When we approach issues with a win–win attitude we ensure that we are part of the solution, not the problem.

Workplaces are complex relationships. And, like all relationships, they can be sick or well. At heart, collaborative processes allow us to find solutions that are better than we as individuals can find on our own. This requires effective communication, understanding each others' perspective, and collaboration to find solutions that are better than any individual team member could come up with alone. As a family is the container for the individual members, so too a workplace culture is the container for its employees.

People who come for therapy often describe themselves as 'conflict avoidant'. However, when they are able to see the costs of this avoidance, it ultimately becomes less scary to practise dealing with conflict. They learn it is safe to speak up for themselves while also taking into account the other's needs. When we listen respectfully and then request the same in return it is far less likely that others will 'railroad', bully or attack us, which are some of the things that conflict-avoiders fear. When we articulate clearly that we are seeking a solution that works for both parties, it is less likely that others will be dismissive. Even if we feel as if we have been ignored or our concerns have been dismissed, it is possible to state *that* in win–win language. And when we sense into that, we often discover that we have been too willing to placate others to create harmony, and in doing so have dismissed our own thoughts and feelings.

Managing expectations

An essential element of healthy work relationships is managing expectations. A problem arises when expectations are unclear or conflicting. It is also problematic when expectations are unrealistic or simply not achievable. The key is to create clear expectations up front and to check regularly to see that everyone is still on the same page. Creating clear expectations means agreeing ahead of time on the desired result and then letting go of the reins a bit. We can provide guidelines, resources and support when requested, but ultimate accountability lies with the person who has to get the task done.

Communication here is central. Mindfulness helps us remain present and open throughout the day. This helps us communicate more effectively as we learn to speak without judgement and listen attentively. Mindful workplaces have clear, realistic expectations as to who is responsible for which tasks and how they are to be achieved. This sets workers up for success.

Having a vision and a clearly articulated mission also helps manage expectations. It contributes to a healthy work culture and sets out what the workplace is trying to achieve. For example, criticism, backstabbing and putting others down creates fear and uncertainty and is destabilizing. So too is micromanaging. Mindful presence facilitates open and honest communication that is founded on respect and self-awareness and allows for individuals to build the bridge of empathy in a work context. This creates a supportive work environment. The qualities of presence and awareness that emanate from people who practice mindfulness make the workplace a positive and nurturing environment.

Learning from failure

Another huge benefit of being mindful at work is the capacity it facilitates to learn from failure. We are often so harshly critical of ourselves and the inner judge (or superego, to use the psychoanalytic term) can be relentless. The biggest problem with this is that as soon as we judge something as bad, we naturally want to avoid it. We then don't take the time to look closely at it, which is necessary if we want to learn from things that don't work. Mindfulness helps here, by teaching us to set aside judgements and to see things on their merits, as they are. Being self-compassionate (and extending this to others) when mistakes are made facilitates this process even more. When we are able to do this, rather than seeing mistakes as disasters they become learning opportunities. Thomas Edison, in trying to find the correct metal for the filament of light globes, is reputed to have tried 10,000 different methods before he came across tungsten. He reportedly said, 'I have not failed. I have just found 10,000 ways that won't work', which perfectly encapsulates the non-judgemental attitude we are talking about here. Imagine if he had beaten himself up after each failure — he would have quit after the first ten and we would be sitting here in the dark!

Mindfulness also helps us step back and see the big picture. This allows us to recognize the context and patterns that give rise to difficulties and failures, as well as seeing what contributes to success. Learning from failure is central to successful workplaces. The openness and presence mindfulness gives us are as essential in the workplace as they are in intimate relationships.

EXERCISE: TRANSFORMING DIFFICULTIES AT WORK

Bring to mind an experience at work or with a group that you would like to change. Sense inwards to see what would feel like a good aspiration to have about the situation. Perhaps you want to speak up or stop being a victim or express some truth. Perhaps you want to be able to see a particular person or situation with compassion.

Now breathe and relax as you notice and connect to this aspiration. Spend a few minutes really holding this aspiration in a heartfelt way.

Come back to it again at another time and notice if it changes. Doing this over and over allows us to get a felt sense of how we would like to be rather than ruminating on things not being as we wish.

CHAPTER 16
Mindful leadership

Modern business practices have seen a move away from formal, linear 'management' and toward leadership. Rather than a strictly defined hierarchy where orders are passed down the chain and carried out in a military fashion, many modern businesses are now encouraging managers to communicate their vision to their employees and encourage genuine buy-in rather than just obedience. When this occurs, each member of a team becomes inspired to add their own unique contribution, while simultaneously being aware of the overall vision of the business or organizational unit they are part of.

Leading effectively in this way demands highly refined emotional intelligence and communication skills. It requires that leaders have a clear sense of their own vision and values, and that they are able to express this vision clearly, in a way that excites and motivates their teams. Effective leadership also necessitates effective conflict resolution skills and that you are able to manage your own stress so that you respond to situations consciously rather than reacting. As you will have realized from previous chapters, mindfulness lies at the heart of these capacities, and can also be used to refine and develop them.

The emotionally intelligent leader

In the book *Emotional Intelligence*, Daniel Goleman spawned a new understanding of what makes someone intelligent. In addition to more traditional notions of intelligence, such as those tapped by a standard IQ test, Goleman's research led us to understand that capacities such as self-awareness, the ability to delay gratification and think before acting, passion for one's work, the ability to understand the emotions and motivations of others and the ability to effectively manage relationships are just as important predictors of success. In fact, emotional intelligence may be even more so — research shows that emotional intelligence is more predictive of academic achievement at university than IQ, and in the 'marshmallow test', four-year-old children who were able to wait five minutes without eating a marshmallow placed in front of them were later found to have significantly higher academic and occupational achievement, better mental health and social wellbeing and fewer criminal convictions than kids who were unable to resist.[1,2]

These emotional intelligence capacities are central to effective leadership. Simply ordering subordinates to carry out specified tasks doesn't require a great deal of understanding of what makes them tick. But getting employees on board with a vision to the extent that they take it on as their own — that is an entirely different story. Mindfulness helps us to slow down and take note of what is happening within and around us. When we pay attention, we can begin to notice how we are feeling in each moment and the way this influences our leadership. We start to notice the effect of our words on others, and whether they are receiving the intended messages. We can recognize our own impulsiveness and remember to pause before acting, so that we can remain responsive rather than becoming reactive. We can tap into our own vision and enthusiasm, and find ways of communicating this. And tuning in to the motivations and values of our team members helps us to understand how best to capitalize on their unique personalities and skills to create strong, productive and happy teams.

In addition, when we develop intimacy with our own inner world and learn to hold our emotions and vulnerabilities in a loving, respectful space, we become able to do this with others. Bringing an attitude of unconditional friendliness to our employees when they are feeling vulnerable reassures them that they can be human and honest about their mistakes and fears, rather than trying to hide them or becoming perfectionistic and stiff in an attempt to compensate for them. When our employees are open with us and comfortable in this way, we are more likely to know where they are at from moment to moment and can respond in a supportive and appropriate way.

Values

One of the most important aspects of leadership is knowing what our values are. Values help to guide our behaviours. They are directions we head in and they help inform our goal setting. Mindfulness helps us sense our way inside and get in touch with what is really important to us. Sometimes we can work out rationally what our values are, but often it is better to become really quiet and still and sense into what is already there. Our values form early in life and then act as both moral compasses and filters, operating largely in the background, outside conscious awareness. This can be very useful, as it frees us up to focus on other things in front of our nose. They keep us heading in the right direction and let us know when we have gone off course.

However, there are times when it can be very valuable to consciously know — and explicitly state — what our values are. In a business context, it can be extremely useful to know how our own values fit with those of the people we work with — therefore knowing where the common ground is, as well as potential sources of conflict. Sometimes we even have conflicting values within ourselves. For instance, we might value health, but simultaneously value having freedom and autonomy — and therefore keep eating whatever we please. Similarly, a business might value the wellbeing of its staff but also profit, which can lead to internal conflict. In these cases, mindfulness can help us to become aware of this internal conflict and to ensure that neither value gets to call all the shots. Rather, we can more consciously use each part of our personality at the appropriate time. For instance, there will be times when discipline and self-control are called for, and others where it can be more useful to relax and go with the flow.

EXERCISE: KNOWING YOUR VALUES

There are a number of ways to gain clarity on what your values are. Here are three of the most effective:

1. Draw up a 2x2 grid and write one of these four headings at the top of each box: personal, social, work, community. Then brainstorm and write down what values you have around each of these. What do you find important? Keep checking to ensure you are writing down values rather than goals: if they are things you can complete and tick off a list, these are goals; if they are aspirations and directions you can head in (but never get to),

these are values. Keep checking in with your body — when you are in touch with your values, this *feels* somehow 'right'. You will feel relaxed and excited at the same time. Use your body sensations to guide you.

2. Imagine your funeral. This is a bit of an odd one, but it can be quite powerful. Really imagine the funeral service, with people standing around your grave or giving speeches in the service. What would you like them to be saying about you? What do you want to be remembered for? What is it that you would like to have contributed to the world? You might even be able to distil it down to one single value, which you might imagine written on your headstone. Then think of ways you can start to express these values while you are still alive.

3. The above two exercises are more conceptual and rational. What can also be very helpful is to use mindfulness to do a non-cognitive inquiry into your values. By this, we mean taking a moment to get into your body and letting go of the busyness of your thoughts — including the ones that are trying to work out what your values are! Get in touch with the stillness that is there and rest in that for a moment. Then drop into that stillness the inquiry, 'What is most important to me?' Allow this question to sit there, to bounce around inside. Don't try to get an answer. Instead, allow one to arise naturally in its own time. Sometimes this happens immediately, and other times it takes a lot longer. Sometimes you might not get an answer at all, but if you leave this inquiry sitting there in that space of stillness, a genuine answer has the chance to arise from deep inside. Just as we sometimes remember someone's name the moment we relax and stop trying to figure it out, so too can true insights into our deepest values arise when we stop trying to work out what they are!

You might like to combine these exercises or do them individually. Experiment and play and find out what works best for you.

Vision

When we know our own values and those of our teams, we can start forming a clear vision that effectively expresses them. Being able to think creatively is central here. We need to be aware of limiting beliefs so they don't impair our vision creation. Carol Dweck, in her book *Mindsets*, talks about 'fixed' and 'growth' mindsets. Fixed mindsets are assumptions about the way things are, should be done and will always be. 'I am a terrible singer' is an example of a fixed mindset and people who hold this belief are likely to avoid any opportunities to sing, denying themselves an opportunity to prove themselves wrong — or at least practise and improve. In contrast, growth mindsets reflect a willingness to investigate how things really *are* and to explore possibilities around what is possible. Some mindfulness teachers refer to this as 'beginner's mind'. As expressed by Zen Master Shunryo Suzuki: 'In the beginner's mind there are many possibilities, but in the expert's there are few.'

Growth mindsets entail an attitude of openness, which is exactly what mindfulness helps us develop. It involves a constant discovery of where we are holding on and limiting ourself, moment by moment, belief by belief. Once we notice a limiting belief or idea, we can let it go. And then for a moment we are free, until we bump into the next limitation.

Another skill central to forming a vision is being able to hold different ideas in mind long enough to see them clearly, critically evaluate them and familiarize ourselves with their intricacies. The ability to keep an image or thought in mind and deal with inevitable distractions is another application of mindfulness. In the beginning, mindfulness practice entails keeping the attention anchored in the five senses, but once this is established we can extend this same quality of awareness to our thoughts. Being able to do this results in clairvoyance, which literally means 'clear seeing' but can take on supernatural qualities when done effectively. Think of business visionaries like Bill Gates and Steve Jobs — they seem to have a 'sixth sense' for what they do, although really this probably reflects more their ability to tap into their own intuition and hold ideas and visions clearly in mind long enough to work out how to achieve them.

EXERCISE: FORMING A CLEAR VISION

Take a few moments to sit and allow the mind to settle. Drop into your body and relax. Get in touch with the breath, resting the attention gently there while it comes and goes.

Once the mind starts to settle, bring to mind something you would like to achieve. Perhaps start with something simple that is easy to imagine. Be curious about how your values can find expression through this vision. Really allow yourself to imagine it in full colour, as clearly as possible. You might see yourself in the future, where that vision has been realized. Notice how it feels in your body, how it sounds. Who else is there, involved in that vision? What can you hear? Can you smell or taste success?

Any time you get distracted by other thoughts, simply let them go and redirect your attention to the vision you were focused on before you got distracted. If you find you get lost in your thoughts, perhaps come to the breath for a time until your mind starts to settle, and then return to the vision once more.

As you get increasingly clear on your vision, tune in to the body sensations that are showing up. The more personally meaningful this vision is to you on the deepest level, the more relaxed and excited you will feel. Really let yourself enjoy these sensations. Doing this will anchor the vision more in your mind, and will motivate you to achieve it (much more than just imagining it).

Communication

Once we have become familiar with our values and vision, we need to be able to communicate these in a way that others can understand and that inspires them to join us in achieving them. Mindful communication involves, as you might imagine, being able to speak and listen mindfully. The default mode of speaking is to chatter without much awareness of what we are saying. If we pay attention, we recognize that our speech is usually laden with self-criticism, judgement and untested assumptions. Having recognized this, we can start speaking mindfully — that is, describing what is actually happening rather than our interpretation of it. It is hard for employees or colleagues to argue with reality, and very easy for them to disagree with our opinions. So speaking in this more mindful way makes for more effective communication.

On the other side of communication, of course, is listening. Here, the default is to half-listen while waiting for our turn to speak, or to zone out completely. Or we may listen, but with judgement. Mindful listening entails really listening to the sounds and the words, rather than to our own judgements about these things.

EXERCISE: BASIC MINDFUL COMMUNICATION

Sit down facing someone and have a conversation. You might like to allow the conversation to happen organically or you might like to choose a speaker and a listener, and for the speaker to talk about something they are interested in and can speak about easily, while the listener listens attentively.

Just have a chat, rather than making this into a formal exercise. However, keep in mind the principles of mindfulness we just mentioned — specifically, awareness and non-judgement. So if you are the speaker, notice if you are really saying what you want to say, or if you are just chattering mindlessly. If you are just chattering, pause for a moment, sense your body, and then start talking again.

Notice too whether there are any judgements in what you are saying. Try to let go of these and just describe things as they are. Likewise, if there are any assumptions you are making, become aware of these too and see if you can describe things accurately.

If you are the listener, your job is just to listen without offering advice or interrupting. Feel free to ask questions and give verbal and nonverbal encouragement to continue, as you would in any conversation. And also be aware that only 20 per cent of communication is verbal (the words that are said). The other 80 per cent is nonverbal — body language, facial expression, gestures, eye contact, tone of voice, rate and volume of speech, prosody (the 'musicality' of speech). Try to listen with all of your senses rather than just your ears. When we really tune in we can even start intuitively getting a 'felt sense' of what our partner is saying.

After a few minutes of doing this, switch roles so that you both get a chance to be the listener and the speaker.

If you want to up the ante a little, try the following:

Again, sit across from someone and decide who will be the listener and speaker. This time, the listener's job is to listen without responding in any way. Just sit and listen. You will notice the automatic tendency to speak or use gestures. As best you can, just let these urges come and go and simply listen. It will most probably get uncomfortable for both of you, but just experiment playfully and see what you can learn from the experience. At the very least, you will see how hard it is to just sit and listen. Sometimes, once the initial discomfort settles, people find they start communicating on a much deeper level.

The speaker's job here is to really express their truth. To do this, it will be necessary to first pause and sense inside. Get yourself quiet and embodied. Then drop into that space the inquiry 'What do I really want to say here?' Sit with that inquiry and allow the answer to arise from somewhere deep inside rather than trying to figure it out. Then, after it has arisen, find words for it and speak it. After you have spoken, pause again and check if those words you just uttered feel right. Do they have integrity? Did you express what you really wanted to say? Have you spoken your truth?

Words can only ever be an approximation and can never fully capture any idea. You will see that clearly when you do this exercise. And so communication becomes an exercise in expressing what is true *as best you can*, while acknowledging this limitation.

After you have checked in and sensed what is true, speak again. Then pause and check the integrity of *that* statement.

While this exercise may seem clunky and artificial at first, with practice it will become more natural. Along the way you will discover what gets in the way of communicating clearly and effectively. And you will start to learn how to truly express your values and vision. You might like to try this exercise with your staff, or weave its principles into your meetings.

Creating a mindful society

As more and more people become aware of the benefits of mindfulness, it has spread beyond medicine and healthcare into business, sport and education. Some people are beginning to wonder what it would look like to create a mindful society. And we don't need to look very far to see that our world certainly needs it! A collective unconsciousness has led to the degradation of the environment, and fight/flight reactivity on a large scale regularly leads to conflict and war. Mindfulness offers a powerful way to start addressing some of these issues.

Each of us is responsible for creating this change. As we have seen throughout *Mindful Relationships*, only when we learn to bring mindfulness and loving presence to ourselves are we able to extend that out towards others. These ripples then travel further and further, meeting other ripples on the way, and mindfulness eventually crosses the whole pond. We create a mindful society by creating a mindful self.

Being the change

Mindfulness starts with being. Only when we learn to quieten down and become intimate with ourselves and the world around us can we start responding appropriately. Prior to that, we are merely reacting. But once we learn how to be, we can discover how to bring that being into the world — into our work and play, into our relationships, families and communities. Doing this effectively requires that we look deeply and see clearly. When we do this, we get to know our core values and deepest desires, and to notice the 'still inner voice' of intuition. And we become able to truly listen and recognize the impact of our words and actions on everything around us.

It is easy to get disheartened by feeling as if we alone have to carry the burden of responsibility for changing the world. We can become overwhelmed by global poverty, high rates of suicide in the young and all the other inequality and injustice in the world. But mindfulness is not necessarily about going out and single-handedly trying to change everything. We may end up doing just this when we hear a calling from deep inside to make a contribution. But it is vital that we don't lose touch with our own heart and become separated from those around us if we do. So much activism today creates further divisions rather than healing by increasing the sense of 'us' and 'them'. To be truly effective agents of change, we need to learn to rest in a space of loving presence and find ways of bringing that into being in the world. Which is easier said than done. In fact, nobody can tell you how to do this. We need to discover it for ourselves.

When Gandhi said, 'Be the change you want to see in the world', he motivated all of India to engage in a nonviolent struggle that ultimately achieved Indian independence. On a smaller scale, we can embody mindfulness by the way we are in the workplace and in our relationships and homes. When we get in touch with our true nature through mindfulness, we discover that far from being some apathetic state where we sit around contemplating our navels, it is very much alive. When we get directly in touch with awareness itself (rather than being distracted by its contents), we find that it is inherently joyful, compassionate and fearless. Think of times you have felt completely contented, even just for a moment, and you will recognize these qualities. The first step is to look deeply and to see who we really are. The way we are in the world then becomes an expression of this being-ness. Mindfulness is transforming our being in a way that is enduring so the traits we express in our everyday life become the ripple effect of the state of mindfulness: loving-kindness and non-judgemental friendliness to our inner experience, which builds a moment-by-moment awareness of presence and what is real.

> Once we develop an intimate relationship with all parts of ourselves, this then ripples out to others in ever-expanding circles, ultimately encompassing all of our relationships and the whole of society.

The very words 'creating a mindful society' imply effort and doing which is anathema to what mindfulness is about. Mindfulness is non-dualistic. It does not separate thoughts and actions but rather comes from a profound sense of wholeness, which is enhanced by a deeper connection to our true nature. It is not about effort and achieving. Rather, it is about listening to what is most meaningful for us. This expresses itself through each person individually and then through society collectively. Each individual has a contribution to make in the world. Joining like-minded groups and communities supports our mindfulness practice and contributes toward building a mindful society. However, it is important to do this without getting caught up in a sense of self-importance or being motivated by wanting to prove we are right so we can strengthen our ego. This is not what mindfulness is about. If we seek to dominate with the importance of our beliefs we make mindfulness just another dogma. Mindfulness continues to come back to the expression of our inner truth as it arises moment by moment, day by day. Whether you are a dentist or a social worker, a factory worker, an insurance broker or a stay-at-home parent, the ripples that you create by relating mindfully to the people and things around you will reverberate and keep on reverberating. If the world is going to genuinely heal and experience less violence and separation and more love, unity and sanity, the change must start with us: each one of us.

We are now aware of our effect on the planet in a way we were not, even just twenty years ago. Our planet is threatened in so many ways and those of us lucky enough to live in parts of the world that are relatively free and developed need to be the change. This requires both rational problem-solving and also developing our compassion and loving presence. We need to shed outdated mindsets and ways of being if we are going to make lasting change. Albert Einstein summed this up when he said, 'We can't solve problems by using the same kind of thinking we used when we created them.' We must be able to sense into the depths of our being, know ourselves fully, and hold all of this in a loving, healing space. Only then will we be able to relate to each other as unique, whole beings and overcome the conflict that results from rejecting parts of ourselves and those around us. When the internal conflict subsides, conflict in the world will subside accordingly. Deep inside each of us is a yearning for this wholeness and loving relationship. All we need to do is listen deeply enough to hear its call, and then follow that.

EXERCISE: WHAT DOES YOUR DEEPEST BEING WANT TO EXPRESS IN THE WORLD?

Take a moment to pause and sense inside. Notice and let go of any tension. Use the breath as an anchor so you can become calm and centred.

Once you start to quieten down ask yourself, 'What do I want to contribute to this world?' or 'What is the next step for me?'

Resist the temptation to try to 'work out' an answer. Instead, allow the question to rest in the stillness as an inquiry. Allow the answer to arise in its own time. Breathe deeply into your belly and let the breath flow throughout your whole body. Cultivate a place of inner stillness and wait. See what arises.

Perhaps for a time nothing will come. Don't judge it if this is the case. Just notice what sensations you are experiencing. Let this question form the basis of an ongoing inquiry.

When answers do arise, simply notice them and check whether they feel true to you. Keep returning to the inquiry.

You might also wish to revisit this inquiry in your daily meditation. When you seek earnestly to know what is your place in this process of building a more mindful society your heartfelt question will connect you with what is most real in you. You will start to be led by intuition and impulses, big and small. Allow these to guide you, always checking back in with yourself as to whether what is arising — and the ways you are bringing it into action — is an expression of mindfulness and loving presence.

Starting where we are

We need to start where we are and be curious about our commitment to relating respectfully and lovingly to all parts of ourself and our world and what this brings. It may calm and focus us. Or it may shake us out of our lethargy and inaction. Little by little, mindfulness takes us on a journey of discovery that expands possibilities beyond what we might previously have considered. Mindfulness is not a quick fix but it necessitates whole-hearted engagement. Mindfulness is inseparable from heartfulness. To quote Eisenstein:

> *Addiction, self-sabotage, procrastination, laziness, rage, chronic fatigue and depression are all ways that we withhold our full participation in the program of life we are offered. When the conscious mind cannot find a reason to say no, the unconscious says no in its own way.*[1]

Mindfulness offers us the capacity to wake up. We begin to see the patterns that may have held us back and the ways in which we have been stuck or saying no to life. Mindfulness allows us to have fresh eyes and to be engaged with life in a fuller way. This requires connecting deeply with an experience of being, and then finding ways to bring that into our doing. It eventually involves changing behaviours, structures and systems where injustice flourishes. What can you do and how can you lend voice to your community, whether it is in prisons, schools, hospitals, with the young or the elderly?

We may very well need to sit with that question as an inquiry, allowing the answer to emerge in its own time from deep inside. The scientific term for humans is Homo Sapiens, meaning 'the ones that have the capacity to know, and to know that they know'. This knowing gives each person immense power, if they are willing and able to use it. A more mindful unfolding in our society will flower and blossom as the ripple effect fans out across the world. As Hugh Mackay says,

> You don't have to be rich to leave a positive legacy; you don't have to be intelligent, famous, powerful or even particularly well organized, let alone happy. You need only to treat people with kindness, compassion and respect, knowing they will have been enriched by their encounters with you.[2]

Picture a society where an understanding and practice of mindfulness is as commonplace as the gym and exercise is to our understanding of health and fitness. Health is not merely the absence of illness. This is why some health insurers have started funding mindfulness classes just as they do for Pilates, yoga and other stress-reduction modalities. Perhaps there will be a juncture between religions and contemplation and mindfulness. We might find the fidelity for our own hearts to live from a place of mindful presence so that we can each bring about a more mindful society. And if it feels as if what you can offer is merely a drop in the ocean of need, remember that oceans are just a lot of drops of water.

ENDNOTES

Chapter 1

1. Richard is a clinical psychologist who sees individual clients, runs mindfulness courses and consults to a growing number of organizations. Margie is a relationship counsellor and communications coach who also works as a family lawyer specializing in collaborative and non-adversarial methods of dispute resolution.

Chapter 2

1. Killingsworth, M.A. and Gilbert, D.T., 'A wandering mind is an unhappy mind', *Science*, 330.6006 (2010): 932.

2. Baumeister, R.F., Finkenauer C. and Vohs, K.D., 'Bad is stronger than good', *Review of General Psychology*, 5(4), 2011:323–70.

3. Zhao, X.H., Wang, P.J., Li, C.B., Hu, Z.H., Xi, Q., Wu, W.Y. and Tang, X.W., 'Altered default mode network activity in patient with anxiety disorders: An fMRI study', *European Journal of Radiology*, 63(3), 2007:373–8.

4. Greicius, M.D., Flores, B.H., Menon, V., Glover, G.H., Solvason, H.B., Kenna, H. and Schatzberg, A.F., 'Resting-state functional connectivity in major depression: Abnormally increased contributions from subgenual cingulate cortex and thalamus', *Biological psychiatry*, 62(5), 2007:429–37.

5. Uddin, L.Q., Kelly, A.M.C., Biswal, B.B., Margulies, D.S., Shehzad, Z., Shaw, D., Ghaffari, M., Rotrosen, J., Adler, L.A., Castellanos, F.X. and Milham, M.P., 'Network homogeneity reveals decreased integrity of default-mode network in ADHD', *J. Neurosci. Methods*, 169, 2008a:249–54.

6. Firbank, M.J., Blamire, A.M., Krishnan, M.S., Teodorczuk, A., English, P., Gholkar, A. and O'Brien, J.T., 'Atrophy is associated with posterior cingulate white matter disruption in dementia with Lewy bodies and Alzheimer's disease', *Neuroimage*, 36(1), 2007:1.

7. Pomarol-Clotet, E., Salvador, R., Sarro, S., Gomar, J., Vila, F., Martinez, A. and McKenna, P.J., 'Failure to deactivate in the prefrontal cortex in schizophrenia: Dysfunction of the default mode network?' *Psychological Medicine*, 38(8), 2008:1185–94.

8. Kennedy, D.P. and Courchesne, E., 'Functional abnormalities of the default network during self- and other-reflection in autism', *Social Cognitive and Affective Neuroscience*, 3(2), 2008:177–90.

9. Michalak, J., Burg, J. and Heidenreich, T., 'Don't forget your body: Mindfulness, embodiment, and the treatment of depression', *Mindfulness*, 3.3, 2012:190–9.

10. Weng, H.Y., Fox, A.S., Shackman, A.J., Stodola, D.E., Caldwell, J.Z., Olson, M.C. and Davidson, R.J., 'Compassion training alters altruism and neural responses to suffering', *Psychological Science*, 24(7), 2013:1171–80.

11. Neff, K.D., 'Self compassion, self-esteem and wellbeing', *Social and Personality Psychology Compass*, 5.1, 2011:1–12.

Chapter 3

1. Monsell, S., 'Task switching', *Trends in Cognitive Sciences*, 7.3. 2003: 134–40.

2. Etkin, A., Egner, T. and Kalisch, R., 'Emotional processing in anterior cingulate and medial prefrontal cortex', *Trends in Cognitive Sciences*, 15.2, 2011:85–93.

3. Goleman, D., *Emotional Intelligence: Why it can matter more than IQ*, 2006, Random House LLC.

4. Staresina, B.P. and Davachi, L., 'Mind the gap: Binding experiences across space and time in the human hippocampus', *Neuron*, 63.2, 2009: 267–76.

5. Lindauer, R.J., Olff, M., van Meijel, E.P., Carlier, I.V. and Gersons, B.P., 'Cortisol, learning, memory, and attention in relation to smaller hippocampal volume in police officers with posttraumatic stress disorder', *Biological Psychiatry*, 59(2), 2006:171–7.

6. Lazar, S.W., Kerr, C.E., Wasserman, R.H., Gray, J.R., Greve, D.N., Treadway, M.T. and Fischl, B., 'Meditation experience is associated with increased cortical thickness', *Neuroreport*, 16(17), 2005:1893.

7. Hölzel, B.K. et al., 'Mindfulness practice leads to increases in regional brain gray matter density', *Psychiatry Research: Neuroimaging*, 19(1), 2011:36–43.

8.   Chambers, R., Lo, B.C.Y. and Allen, N.B., 'The impact of intensive midfulness training on attention control, cognitive style, and affect', *Cognitive Therapy and Research*, 32(3), 2008:303–322.

9.   Keng, S.L, Smoski, M.J. and Robins, C.J., 'Effects of mindfulness on psychological health: A review of empirical studies', *Clinical Psychology Review*, 31.6, 2011:1041–56.

10. Kabat-Zinn, J., 'An outpatient program in behavioral medicine for chronic pain patients based on the practice of mindfulness meditation: Theoretical considerations and preliminary results', *General Hospital Psychiatry*, 4.1, 1982:33–47.

11. Kaplan, K.H., Goldenberg, D.L. and Galvin-Nadeau, M., 'The impact of a meditation-based stress reduction program on fibromyalgia', *General Hospital Psychiatry*, 15.5, 1993: 284–9.

12. Kabat-Zinn, J., loc. cit.

13. Schmidt, S., Simshäuser, K., Aickin, M., Lüking, M., Schultz, C. and Kaube, H., 'Mindfulness-based stress reduction is an effective intervention for patients suffering from migraine: Results from a controlled trial', *European Journal of Integrative Medicine*, 2(4), 2010:196.

14. Kabat-Zinn, J., Wheeler, E., Light, T., Skillings, A., Scharf, M.J., Cropley, T.G. and Bernhard, J.D., 'Influence of a mindfulness meditation-based stress reduction intervention on rates of skin clearing in patients with moderate to severe psoriasis undergoing photo therapy (UVB) and photochemotherapy (PUVA)', *Psychosomatic Medicine*, 60(5), 1998:625–32.

15. Carlson, L.E., Speca, M., Patel, K.D. and Goodey, E., 'Mindfulness-based stress reduction in relation to quality of life, mood, symptoms of stress, and immune parameters in breast and prostate cancer outpatients', *Psychosomatic Medicine*, 65(4), 2003:571–81.

16. Epel, E., Daubenmier, J., Moskowitz, J.T., Folkman, S. and Blackburn, E., 'Can meditation slow rate of cellular aging? Cognitive stress, mindfulness, and telomeres', *Annals of the New York Academy of Sciences*, 2009;1172(1):34–53.

17. Taylor, S.E., Klein, L.C., Lewis, B.P., Gruenewald, T.L., Gurung, R.A. and Updegraff, J.A., 'Biobehavioral responses to stress in females: Tend-and-befriend, not fight-or-flight', *Psychological Review*, 107(3), 2000:411.

18. Hughes, B.L. and Beer, J.S., 'Orbitofrontal cortex and anterior cingulate cortex are modulated by motivated social cognition', *Cerebral Cortex*, 2011: bhr213.

19. Lutz, A., Brefczynski-Lewis, J., Johnstone, T. and Davidson, R.J., 'Regulation

of the neural circuitry of emotion by compassion meditation: Effects of meditative expertise', *PloS One*, 3(3), 2008:e1897.

Chapter 6

1. Lerner, H.G., *The Dance of Intimacy: A woman's guide to courageous acts of change in key relationships*, 1998, HarperCollins New York.

Chapter 8

1. Silverstein, R.G., Brown, A.C.H., Roth, H.D. and Britton, W.B., 'Effects of mindfulness training on body awareness to sexual stimuli: Implications for female sexual dysfunction', *Psychosomatic Medicine*, 73(9), 2011:817.
2. When we refer to a 'partner' we are really referring to one or more intimate or sexual partners, of any gender or sex. We recognize the vast variability of sexual preferences and tastes, including heterosexuality, homosexuality, bisexuality, monogamy and polyamoury.
3. Lindauer, R.J.L, et al. loc. cit.
4. Taylor, S.E., et al. loc. cit.
5. This is a generalization and of course there is infinite variability in both men and women around this. When we refer to 'men' we are really referring to more masculine people, and by 'women' we refer to people who have more strongly developed feminine traits. Therefore, a man with a strongly developed feminine side is likely to value emotional intimacy, while a woman who has a highly developed masculine side is likely to be more able to just 'have sex'.

Chapter 9

1. Gottman, J.M. and Levenson, R.W., 'The timing of divorce: Predicting when a couple will divorce over a fourteen year period', *Journal of Marriage and Family*, 62.3, 2000: 737–45.

Chapter 13

1. Covey, S.R., *The 7 Habits of Highly Effective Families*, Allen & Unwin, 1997, Sydney.
2. http://www.nydailynews.com/life-style/average-american-watches-5-hours-tv-day-article-1.1711954

3. Mayo Clinic, 'Children and TV: Limiting your child's screen time', 2014, cited at http://www.mayoclinic.org/healthy-lifestyle/childrens-health/in-depth/children-and-tv/art-20047952

4. Christakis, D.A., Zimmerman, F.J., DiGiuseppe, D.L. and McCarty, C.A., 'Early television exposure and subsequent attentional problems in children', *Pediatrics*, 113(4), 2004:708–13.

5. Lillard, A.S. and Peterson, J., 'The immediate impact of different types of television on young children's executive function', *Pediatrics*, published online 12 September 2011, (doi: 10.1542/peds. 2010-1919).

6. Lindstrom, H.A., Fritsch, T., Petot, G., Smyth, K.A., Chen, C.H., Debanne, S.M. and Friedland, R.P., 'The relationships between television viewing in midlife and the development of Alzheimer's disease in a case-control study', *Brain and Cognition*, 58(2), 2005:157–65.

7. Halayem, S., Nouira, O., Bourgou, S., Bouden, A., Othman, S. and Halayem, M., 'The mobile: A new addiction upon adolescents', *La Tunisie Medicale*, 88(8), 2010:593–6.

8. Angster, A., Frank, M. and Lester, D., 'An exploratory study of students' use of cell phones, texting, and social networking sites', *Psychol Rep.*, 2010;107:402–4, cited at http://www.ncbi.nlm.nih.gov/pubmed/21117464.

9. Phipps-Nelson, J., Redman, J.R., Schlangen, L.J. and Rajaratnam, S.M., 'Blue light exposure reduces objective measures of sleepiness during prolonged nighttime performance testing', *Chronobiology International*, 26(5), 2009:891–912.

10. Gradisar, M., Wolfson, A.R., Harvey, A.G., Hale, L., Rosenberg, R. and Czeisler, C.A., 'The sleep and technology use of Americans: Findings from the National Sleep Foundation's 2011 "Sleep in America" poll', *J Clin Sleep Med*, 9(12), 2013:1291–9.

11. http://www.aap.org/en-us/advocacy-and-policy/aap-health-initiatives/Pages/Media-and-Children.aspx

Chapter 14

1. McEvoy, S.P., Stevenson, M.R. and Woodward, M., 'The prevalence of, and factors associated with, serious crashes involving a distracting activity', *Accident Analysis & Prevention*, 39.3, 2007: 475–82.

2. Hickman, J.S. and Hanowski, R.J., 'An assessment of commercial motor vehicle driver distraction using naturalistic driving data', *Traffic Injury Prevention*, 13.6, 2012: 612–19.

3. Slagter, H.A., Lutz, A., Greischar, L.L., Francis, A.D., Nieuwenhuis, S., Davis, J.M. and Davidson, R.J., 'Mental training affects distribution of limited brain resources', *PLoS Biology*, 5(6), 2007:e138.

4. Jackson, T.W., Dawson, R. and Wilson, D., 'The cost of email within organizations', *Strategies for eCommerce Success*, 2002:307.

5. Wilson, G., 'Infomania experiment for HP', cited at http://www.governmentinfopro.com/files/weldonarticle2010.pdf

6. Dr Clifford Nass of Stanford University. From Dretzin, R. and Rushkoff, D., 'Digital nation life on the virtual frontier', pbs.org Frontline, cited 14 April 2011.

7. Wetherell, M.A. and Carter, K., 'The multitasking framework: The effects of increasing workload on acute psychobiological stress reactivity', *Stress and Health*, 30.2, 2014:103–9.

8. Ashcraft, M.H. and Kirk, E.P., 'The relationships among working memory, math anxiety, and performance', *Journal of Experimental Psychology: General*, 130.2, 2001:224.

9. Liston, C., McEwen, B.S. and Casey, B.J., 'Psychosocial stress reversibly disrupts prefrontal processing and attentional control', *Proceedings of the National Academy of Sciences*, 106.3, 2009: 912–17.

10. Lindauer, R.J.L. et al. loc. cit.

11. Zeidan F., Johnson, S.K., Diamond, B.J., David, Z. and Goolkasian, P., 'Mindfulness meditation improves cognition: Evidence of brief mental training', *Conscious Cogn.*, 2010 Jun;19(2):597–605. Epub 2010 Apr 3.

12. Chambers, R., Lo, B.C.Y. and Allen, N.B., 'The impact of intensive mindfulness training on attentional control, cognitive style, and affect', *Cognitive Therapy and Research*, 32(3), 2008:303–22.

13. De Neys, W., Vartanian, O. and Goel, V., 'Smarter than we think: When our brains detect that we are biased', *Psychological Science*, 19.5, 2008: 483–9.

14. Ludwig, D.S. and Kabat-Zinn, J., 'Mindfulness in medicine', *JAMA*, 300.11, 2008:1350–2.

15. Hayes, A.M. and Feldman, G., 'Clarifying the construct of mindfulness in the context of emotion regulation and the process of change in therapy', *Clinical Psychology: Science and Practice*, 11.3, 2004:255–62.

16. Krasner, M.S., Epstein, R.M., Beckman, H., Suchman, A.L., Chapman, B., Mooney, C.J. and Quill, T.E., 'Association of an educational program in mindful communication with burnout, empathy, and attitudes among primary care physicians', *JAMA*, 302(12), 2009:1284–93.

17. Greenberg, J., Reiner, K. and Meiran, N., '"Mind the trap": Mindfulness practice reduces cognitive rigidity', *PLoS One*, 2012:7(5):e36206. Epub 15 May 2012.

Chapter 16

1. Parker, J.D., Summerfeldt, L.J., Hogan, M.J. and Majeski, S.A., 'Emotional intelligence and academic success: Examining the transition from high school to university', *Personality and Individual Differences*, 36(1), 2004:163–72.

2. Mischel, W., Shoda, Y. and Rodriguez, M.I., 'Delay of gratification in children', *Science*, 244.4907, 1989: 933–8.

Epilogue

1. Eisenstein, C., *The More Beautiful World Our Hearts Know Is Possible*, 2013, North Atlantic Books, Berkeley.

2. Mackay, H., *The Good Life: What makes a life worth living?* 2013, Pan MacMillan, Sydney.

INDEX

A

acceptance, meaning of 120–1
'activation response' 28
activities
    everyday 17
    mindful 10–11
addiction to smartphones 182
ADT ('Attention Deficit Trait') 190
amygdala, diagram 27
'amygdala hijack' 28
anger
    a cover up 60–1
    covers vulnerability 95
    recognizing 94
    repeating parent's 150
    triggers 95
    wisdom of 80
anxious/ambivalent attachment 146
apologizing 124
attachment styles 146–7
attention, paying 18–19
'Attention Deficit Trait' (ADT) 190
attentional blink 189–90
automatic pilot 14
avoidance
    pattern of 122
    strategies 72–3
avoidant attachment 146
awareness
    developing 19–20
    of family feelings 175
    introceptive 103

B

bedtime, as a threat 150
'beginner's mind' 193
biases
    impair decision-making 193
    negativity bias 13
'bids for contact' 86–8
blame
    coping strategy 117–18
    futility of 133–6
    stopping 91
boundaries
    establishing and maintaining 149–50
    technology use 180–4
Brach, Tara 48
brain development, children's 151–3
brain rewiring 25–6
breastfeeding, resentment about 158–9
breath, noticing 21–2
breathing, basic meditation 42
Brown, Brené 118

C

calming down 94–5
Carol and Jack
    awareness of own contributions 124
    cycle of recrimination 122–3
    take responsibility 125–6
change, being the change 216–19
childhood, wounds from 124
children
    brain development 151–3
    closer to one parent 148
    criticism from parents 124
    encouraging meditation 161–5
    expecting criticism 151
    experiencing *vs* acting out 144
    lack of love 149–50
    learning from failure 153–4
    mindful meditation practices 161–5
    mindfulness games 163–5
    naming emotions 144
    need for loving presence 100–1
    position in family 174
    relationship with parents 146–8
    sit with their emotions 145
    vulnerability of 143–6
Chödron, Pema 75, 118
cognitive emotions 20
collective unconsciousness, damage by 215
Colleen, sex therapy 112–13
communication
    effective 92–6
    enhancing 62
    within family 173
    open and honest 175
    timing of 93
    of values and vision 210–13
    workplace expectations 199
compassion
    friendly 123
    relationship benefits 100–3
    unconditional 90
    wrathful 145
concrete operational stage 152–3
confirmation biases 193
conflict
    avoiding 198
    cycle of 122–3
    in relationships 6, 127
conflict resolution 196
contact, bids for 86–8
contempt, and divorce 119
cortisol 28
couple's therapy 132
criticism
    children expecting 151

from parents 124
crying, stages of 143–4
curiosity 21–3

D
The Dance of Intimacy (book) 72
daydreaming 15
death, handling 154–5
decision-making 193
default mode
    to avoid or control 72
    effect on happiness 12–13
    explained 12–14
    noticing 22
    recognizing 16
    self-criticism 23
differentiated stance 135–6
differentiation
    explained 97–100
    lack of 98
difficulties, trying to avoid 6
disagreement
    interpreting opinions 210
    reacting to 92
discernment counselling 132–3
discomfort, inevitable 48, 57
disorganized attachment 147
divorce
    children's reaction 154–5
    contempt factor 119
downtime, importance of 194
driving, and phone conversations 188
Dweck, Carol 208

E
eating
    on automatic pilot 14
    mindful 18, 64
Edison, Thomas 200
Einstein, Albert 218
Eisenstein, C 220
electronic devices 181–3
email
    limit checking 192
    overnight shut down 194
embodiment 20–1
emotions
    children learn to sit with 145
    children naming them 144
    common primary 60
    cut off from 75
    'feeding or fighting' 60–2
    feeling full range of 91
    learning to tolerate 95–6
    managing difficult ones 55–62
    numbing 72–3
    observing 7
    secondary 60

source of wisdom 95
transience of 101
tuning in to 20
unpleasant 48
work at three levels 61
young children 100–1
empathy 100–3
empty nesters
    no conversation 92–3
    transition years 98
enlightenment 48–9
erection, difficulty with 113–14
exercises
    accessing wisdom to change patterns 177
    activating our tend-and-befriend circuits 109–10
    basic mindful communication 211–12
    basic mindfulness meditation 42–3
    body as an anchor 16–17
    body as guide to behaviour 166–7
    bringing a friendly presence 88–9
    contacting awareness 19
    contacting the loving presence 76–7
    creating mindful families 178
    developing empathy 102–3
    expressing deepest want 219
    forming a clear vision 209–10
    grounding and self-soothing 31–2
    hugging meditation 103
    knowing what you want 137
    knowing your family 174
    knowing your values 206–8
    learning how to fight fair 129
    learning to unitask 191–2
    listening deeply 102–3
    loving ourselves and others 82–3
    loving-kindness meditation 33–5
    meditating on your child/teenager 159–60
    mindful of everyday practices 52
    mindful self-care 66
    noticing resistance 58
    noticing the attentional blink 189
    observing relationships 7–8
    recognizing mindful moments 11–12
    savouring positive experiences 168–9
    sensing deepest longing for family 176
    slowing down and connecting during sex 114–15
    speaking from the heart 96
    transforming difficulties at work 201
expectations
    letting go of 86
    managing 199
    realistic 150–3
eye contact, while fighting 128

F

failure
    children learning from 153–4
    learning from 200
family
    container for development 172–5
    creating mindful families 178
    healthy relationships 175–6
    intimacy/connection with 171–2
    trust in relationship 173
family culture 175–80
feeling emotions 20
feelings
    acknowledging 94
    taking responsibility for 100
fight/flight mode
    amygdala activated 28
    blood flow 108
    crying children 143–4
    permission to go into 119
fighting fair 127–9
Fischer, Janine 119
fixed mindsets 193, 208
formal operational stage 153
Full Catastrophe Living (book) 23–4

G

games, mindfulness 163–5
Gandhi 7, 216
gentleness 22–3
Gilbert, Daniel 12
Goleman, Daniel 204
Gottman, John 86–7, 119, 127, 131
gratification 67
grief, handling 154–5
growth mindsets 208
The Guest House (poem) 80–1

H

half-listening 210
happiness, three types of 67
healing, true meaning of 80
health, improving 29
health insurers, funding mindfulness classes 221
health problems, default mode association 13
heartfulness *see* self-compassion
help, when and how to seek 131–3
hippocampus, diagram 27

I

iceberg metaphor for family 173
ideas, holding differing 208–9
individuality, fostering 148–9
infants, dependence of 146
informal practice
    applying mindfulness 51–5
    everyday activities 17–18
    list of examples 53–4

insula, diagram 27
intelligence, new understanding of 204
intimacy
    developing 7
    explained 71–2
    lack of 5–6
    with our family 171–2
    reconnecting 75–6
    repair ruptures in 119–21
    sexual 106
    what it is 81, 85
introceptive awareness 107

J

Jane and Michael
    'bids for contact' 87
    stop blaming 91
judgement, less *see* non-judgement
Jung, Carl 57, 89

K

Kabat-Zinn, Jon 7, 23–4, 47–8
Killingsworth, Matthew 12

L

leadership
    effective 203
    emotionally intelligent 204–5
    values 205–8
legacy, leaving a positive one 221
Lerner, Harriet 72
letting go 86
liberation, path to 6–7
lifestyle, sustainable, nourishing 63–5
listening
    deeply 102–3
    mindful 210
loss, handling 154–5
love
    natural flow of 149
    what it is 85
lovemaking meditation 111
loving presence
    for childhood emotions 144–5
    children's need for 100–1
    developing 74–6
loving-kindness 30–5

M

Mackay, Hugh 221
MBCT (Mindfulness-Based Cognitive
    Therapy) 44
MBSR (Mindfulness-Based Stress
    Reduction) 44
meditation
    benefits of 39–41
    exercise for parents 159–60
    hugging exercise 103

lovemaking meditation 111
practice tips 161–2
regular practice 43–6
tips for 45
see also mindfulness meditation
mental health
default mode association 13
improving 29
mind wandering *see* default mode
mindful activities 10–11
'mindful muscle', building 29
mindfulness
better sex 109–11
central qualities 18–24
classes funded 221
cultivating 3–4
embodying 157–61
an everyday experience 10–11, 54–5
explained 9–10
games 163–5
is 'tuning in' 46–8
as a practice 15–16
mindfulness meditation 15, 41–3, 161–5
Mindfulness-Based Cognitive Therapy (MBCT) 44
Mindfulness-Based Stress Reduction (MBSR) 44
mindsets
fixed 193, 208
growth 208
open 193
outdated 218
movie analogy, pause for reality check 63–4
multitasking
myth of 188–91
time lost to 190

N
needs
directly expressing 94
see also differentiation
Neff, Kristin 48
negativity bias 13
neuroplasticity
lovemaking and 111
rewiring the brain 25–6
non-judgement
central to mindfulness 22
mitigates unpleasantness 46
in parenting 151

O
object permanence 152
open mindsets 193
Ornish, Dean 85
ourselves, learning to love 78–80

P
parenting
challenges of 141–2

mindful 150
unified 147–8
parents
discussing differences 148
fail to comfort child 101–2
not unified 147–8
repeating own experience 150
wrathful compassion 145–6
partners
getting to therapy 133–6
listening to perspective 134
pausing
learning 98–9
for reality check 63–4
paying attention, to resolve conflict 127
personality, 'shadow' aspects 89
physical exercise 11, 65
Piaget, Jean 151–2
pleasing others, pattern of 149–50
'positive psychology' 67
power, responsibility and awareness of 117–19
Practicing Peace (book) 118
prefrontal cortex
activated 47
diagram 27
executive functioning 26–7
preoperational stage 152
present moment
effects of staying in 120
living fully in 67
see also mindfulness
projection
reaction to partner 89
recognizing 91
pursuer–distancer pattern 124

R
reality, accepting 90
rejection, stuck in patterns 123
relationship difficulties, seeking help 131–3
relationships
children with parents 146–8
'drowning' in 97
as an entity 125
imagining yours 136
inevitable disappointment 48
no-negativity zone 128
past traumas 87
path to healing 75–6
reasons for failure 86
unresolved issues 108
see also workplaces
re-parenting ourselves 142, 146, 147
resilience 153–5
resistance
common forms of 57

letting go of 55–62
masquerading as acceptance 47
responsibility, for own part 126–7
responsible citizens, raising 165–8
Rumi (poet) 80–1

S

Sarah, work stress 56–9
Schnarch, David 97
secure attachment 146
self
looking deeply into 89–92
losing sense of 97–8
loving ourselves 78–80
self-care 63–6
self-compassion
central quality 48
explained 23–4
giving insulation 30–1
healing ability 73–4
self-criticism 23
self-worth, shaped by family 172–3
Seligman, Martin 67
sensorimotor stage 151–2
separateness, respect for 148–9
separations, mindful 136
sex
as communication 107
dissociation during 107–8
mindful 109–11
reliving the experience 105–6
slowing down and connecting exercise 114–15
sex life, healthy 107–9
sex therapy 112–13
sexual issues, resolving 112–15
'shadow' aspect, personality 89
'signature strengths' 67
Simon, sex therapy 113–14
sleep, individual needs 64–5
smartphones
effect on behaviour 181–3
mealtime rules 183
smothered, feeling 97
society, mindful 215
Socrates 91
somatic emotions 20
space, asking for and taking 121–7
spiritual bypassing 6
stress
reducing 55–62
understanding relationship with 55–7
workplace 56–9
stuck, childhood wounds 124

T

technology
managing use of 180–3
mindful use of 183–4

television
impact of watching 181
screen time limits 183–4
'tend-and-befriend' circuits
activating 30
strengthening 109–11
'tender soft spot' 75
therapists, finding 137–8
thinking emotions 20
threats
bedtime 150
modern day 13
nonverbal cues 108
Tim and Amanda
effective communication 93–4
learning to differentiate 98–9
therapy after separation 136
timing of communication 93
Tom, repeats father's anger 150
trauma
dealing with effect 21
past 87
trust, family relationships 173
tuning in
experience of 46–8
to our bodies 20–1

U

unconditional friendliness *see* self-
compassion
understanding, unconditional 90
unified parenting 147–8
unitasking 191–3
unpleasant experiences, cutting off from
72

V

values of leadership 205–8
vision, to express values 208–10
vulnerability
acknowledging our own 89–91
children 143–6
couples sharing 126
covered by anger 95
of partner 103
sensing into our own 118
taking responsibility for 99–100

W

win–win, negotiation 196–8
workplaces
communication within 199
effective leadership 204–5
learning from failure 200
managing expectations 199
negotiating win–win 196–8
stress in 56–9
stress reduction 55–62